# CADOGAN

## Michael Pauls & Dana Facaros

## the travellers' guide to

# HELL

Go to Hell                                    2

Making the Most of Your Eternity    12

Who's Who of Hell                          32

Touring Hell                                   41

Parallel Hells                                   58

Hell through the Ages                     76

D1508712

CADOGAN GUIDES
published by Cadogan Guides
27–29 Berwick Street, London W1V 3RF, UK
e-mail: guides@cadogan.demon.co.uk

distributed in North America by
The Globe Pequot Press
6 Business Park Road, PO Box 833, Old Saybrook,
Connecticut 06475–0833

text © Michael Pauls & Dana Facaros 1998
first published in 1998. ISBN 1-86011-910-7

series directed by Rachel Fielding
editor: Mary-Ann Gallagher
proofreading: Catherine Charles
cover design: Horacio Monteverde
book design: Kicca Tommasi
picture research: Vanessa Letts and Mary-Ann Gallagher
production: Book Production Services
publicity: Antonia McCahon
Printed in Great Britain by WBC Book Manufacturers Ltd.

photographic and picture credits:

p.5. *The Table of the Seven Deadly Sins* by Hieronymous Bosch (c.1450-1516)
Prado, Madrid/Bridgeman Art Library, London/New York
p.74. *The Garden of Earthly Delights: Hell*, c.1500 (panel) by Hieronymous Bosch (c.1450-1516)
Prado, Madrid/Bridgeman Art Library, London/New York
p.75. *The Last Judgement* (details of the Righteous Drawn up to Heaven)) by Michelangelo
Vatican Museum and Galleries, Vatican City/Bridgeman Art Library, London/New York
p.77. *Plaque of Hell, depicting the conspiracy saga against Lamashtu, Neo-Assyrian, from Mesopotamia*, c.1700BC
(bronze). Louvre, Paris/Bridgeman Art Library, London, New York.
p.83. *Hercules and Diamedes* by Baron Antoine Jean Gros (1771-1835)
Musee des Augustins, Toulouse/Giraudon/Bridgeman Art Library, London/New York
p.85. *Orpheus with a Harp Playing to Pluto and Persephone in the Underworld* by Jan the Elder Brueghel
(1563-1625). Johnny van Haeften Gallery, London/Bridgeman Art Library, London/New York
p.85. *The Cuman Sibyl* from Villa Carducci series of Famous Men and Women, c.1450, fresco, by Andrea del
Castagno (1423-57). Galleria degli Uffizi, Florence/Bridgeman Art Library, London/New York
p.86. *Satan Calling Up His Legions* by William Blake (1757-1827)
Victoria and Albert Museum, London/Bridgeman Art Library, London/New York
pp.21, 33. © Ken Brown (*Early to Rise and Hell's Bellbottoms*)
p.62. Courtesy of Boomer Rickets (*Stone Buddha*)
p.73. © Vincent Mentzel (*BB King*)
p.115. © Tri-Star Pictures (*Robert de Niro*)

Every effort has been made to trace the copyright holders and we apologise for any unintentional omissions. We
would be pleased to insert the appropriate acknowledgement in any subsequent edition of this publication.

## about the authors

**Dana Facaros and Michael Pauls**, a pair of experienced old sinners, are seasoned travellers and authors of over thirty infernally good travel guides. Researching this book they have gone to hell and back, returning with barely a scorch mark to their bad old ways of devilry and riotous living. Next time they might try up rather than down… 🖐

## acknowledgements

*To Villia's demonic duo, Michael and Brian, with love and Insanity Sauce kisses.*

Half of this book was written in Greece, and the other half in an attic. Both places were hot as blazes, which certainly helped to set the mood. We're indebted once again to the usual suspects, to Marge Pauls, for the use of the attic, to Chris Malumphy and Carolyn Steiner, and once again, amazingly enough, to Chris's antique 1984 Macintosh, which came out of the bottom of the closet again to write its second book. Also thanks to Lily, who had better clean up her room or else.

If you want to research Hell, you can do worse than come to Cleveland. Our sincere thanks to the exceptional staff of the Cleveland Public Library, to all the good brothers who hand out tracts on Public Square and in the West Side Market parking lot, and to the Rite Aid drug store on Broadview for stocking such a comprehensive selection of trash tabloids. And special thanks to Reverend Odus Lee Wiggins of Bateman, Oklahoma—without Odus to tell us the real story, we might have had to make one up.

The publishers wish to thank all those who dared descend into Hell: in particular, special thanks to Dana and Michael for hours on the coals under our whip; Kicca for her devilish design and the loan of body parts and her halo; Vanessa and Mary-Ann for raking the fiery depths to bring back just the right pictures, hot sauces, sardines, feathers, bikers and fishnet tights; Suzannah and Ed for scouring New York for stylishly satanic tat.

# contents

**Go To Hell**

Before You Go                                    2
What to Pack                                     3
Toilet Facilities                                4
Travel                                           4
Seven Highways to Hell:
    The Deadly Sins                              5
Transportation                                   8
Infernal Geography                              10

**Making the Most
    of Your Eternity**                          12

Your Host                                       12
Calling Home                                    18
Hell's Kitchen: Food and Drink                  19
Entertainment                                   21
Holidays                                        24
Handle with Care                                26
Hell on Wheels                                  30
A Day Trip into Limbo                           30

**Who's Who of Hell**                           32

Abraxas                                         33
Adramalech                                      34
Asmodeus                                        34
Astaroth                                        35
Azazel                                          35
Balam                                           35
Beelzebub                                       36
Belial                                          36
Belphegor                                       37
Incubi                                          37
Lilith                                          38
Mammon                                          39
Mephistopheles                                  39
Sammael                                         40
Succubi                                         40

**Touring Hell**                                41

What's Your Sin, Brother                        42
Dante's and Odus's Hell Gazetteer               43

**Hotel Hells:
    Where to Stay**                             58

Chinese Hell                                    58
Buddhism: Hot Hells and Cold Hells              62
The Islamic Pit                                 64
Viking Hel                                      66
Milton's Inferno: Hell as High Art              68
Bad Bill Blake's Hell for Heroes                69
West Hell                                       72
Hell Sells                                      74

**Hell through the Ages**                       76

Mesopotamians and Egyptians                     76
Zoraster Takes Over                             78
Hades: Hell in Classical Times                  80
Orphic Hell                                     84
A Tour of Roman Hell                            86
Mithraic Hell                                   88
Jewish Sheol and Gehenna                        89
Lucifer Takes a Stand                           90
Christian Hell                                  92
Alexandrian Universalism                        94
The Harrowing of Hell                           95
Last Judgements                                 96
Pick a Number                                   98
Alternative Apocalypses                         99
Alternative Christians                          101
Medieval Hell                                   103
The Reformation                                 107
Hell Today                                      113
The Last True Believers                         116
L'Envoi                                         122

# go to

## Before You Go

It makes sense. If you're going trekking, you take walks around the block to get in shape. If you're visiting coral reefs, you take a scuba course at the local pool. Going to Hell? Not to worry. In the same way that Rome's nemesis, Mithradates of Pontus, took a little venom every day to inoculate himself against the likelihood of a Roman slipping him a mickey, you can prepare for Hell's warm glow, and perhaps even look forward to it by partaking of condiments with names that betray their homeopathic purpose: Jamaica Hell Fire, Sudden Death, Rectal Rocket Fuel, DanT's Inferno, Satan's Breath, Ring of Fire, Viper Venom, or Blair's After Death Sauce. Wash them down with Infernovodka, made from Canadian vodka and red peppers. If you're bad and you know it, you might as well go straight to the big bazooka of gastric ballistics, Dave's Limited Reserve Insanity Sauce (it comes in its own little wooden coffin). After a slurp of Dave's brew, even the hellfire of the Jesuits, 'when every damned person will be like a heated oven, blazing hot on the inside and inside his chest; the filthy blood will boil in his veins, as will the brain in his skull, the heart in his chest, and the guts in his wretched body ...' will seem downright benign. ✺

# HELL

## What to Pack

In the old days, you had to at least take down a coin (two *obols*, worth about a tenner now, what with inflation) with you to pay Charon, the ferryman on the Styx. If you didn't have the fare Charon wouldn't take you, and you would have to spend an eternity moping around the Stygian shore with all the other deadbeats.

These days, you haven't a thing to worry about; free admission was one of the first reforms introduced by the Christians. If you're just going for a short stay, like Dante, pack lightly, and be careful you don't bring back any unwanted souvenirs. An evangelist named Peter Wagner from Birmingham (England, that is, not Alabama) would extend this warning to places on earth. He says demons like to hide in suitcases, and there is a real problem with people bringing them back after visiting the ruins of pagan temples on holiday.

> everything necessary for a happy stay in Hell will be supplied by your hosts

In truth, you can't take it with you, to Heaven or to Hell, but you won't need it. Absolutely everything necessary for a happy stay in Hell will be supplied by your hosts. Leonard Ashley, that careful researcher, wrote (in *The Devil's Disciples*) of an old-time camp meeting down in the Deep South where:

> ...the preacher had taken as his text Matthew 49:50, and was doing a riff on 'weeping and wailing and gnashing of teeth'.
>
> One of the congregation shouted, 'Preacher, I ain't got no teeth!'
>
> 'Brother,' came the reply, 'teeth will be provided.!'

## Toilet Facilities

Make sure you go before leaving home. In Hell, eternal punishment is without relief.

## Travel

As everyone knows, the road there is wide and easy, and paved with good intentions; nobody bound for the place has ever lost their way. Still, you sinners in a hurry can reserve a place in advance by selling your soul to the devil. Old Nick has unbeatable special offers to go with advance bookings—wealth, high office, magic powers, sex, tomatoes that really taste like tomatoes; you name it. If you're short of time, you can sell your soul without leaving home, by e-mail on Hell's homepage *www.sff.net/people/pitman/ hell.htm.* (it also includes Satan's CV and references, so you know exactly whom you're dealing with). There's a form to fill in, listing the most common desires, with the rather limited warranty: 'All Sales Final. No Returns, No Refunds, No Substitutions. A 7% Sales Tax is Applicable in California.' Like most special offers, however, the devil's deals are for a limited period only, usually 7 or 24 years, and when the time's up, you get a free, personal escort service to hell. Thomas Cook and American Express can't begin to compete.

Of course, the devil has more experience than Thomas Cook. His first recorded deal goes back to the 4th or 5th century. Theophilus, Archdeacon of Adana (Turkey), was

# all sales final. no refunds.

# a 7% sales tax is applicable in california

unfairly fired from his post, and went off in a huff; using a sorcerer as a middle man, he sold his soul to the Devil. The ex-Archdeacon enjoyed all the usual privileges before he had an attack of remorse and tried to renegotiate the deal: no dice. Theophilus, however, repented so sincerely that the Virgin Mary took pity on him, and just before the Devil was about to snatch the prize, she went down to hell, grabbed the contract and tore it up, leaving Theophilus to die in an odour of sanctity rather than sulphur. As beloved as she is on earth, the Virgin Mary is *persona non grata* in hell; old central Italian paintings show her as a giantess, walloping the devil with a wooden club when he tries to carry off a baby.

If humans always try to renege, the Devil for his part always keeps his end of the bargain, even to the point of stupidity. All across Europe, rivers are spanned by 'Devil's bridges', thrown up by the devil in a single night, in exchange for the first soul to cross. Every last time clever villagers push a dog or cat over for him to snatch. Even more surprisingly, the Devil builds churches, such as the Cathedral of Aix-la-Chapelle (he got a wolf's soul for that one).

# Seven Highways to Hell: the Deadly Sins

The most entertaining route to Hell is still the old-fashioned way: being bad. The **Seven Deadly Sins** were set up as guidelines to just the kind of misbehaviour required, and by carefully committing the right ones, you may well land that certain place in Hell you really want.

The origins of the Seven are somewhat surprising. In Roman times, Christianity faced some tough competition from other mystery religions. Many of these proffered decent afterlife benefits, but none of them had Christianity's disadvantages in this

Hieronymus Bosch *the Table of the Seven Deadly Sins*

Where there's a will, there's a won't.

*The Devil's Dictionary*

world: namely a chance of being converted into lion fodder. Because of this handicap, the early Christians reverted to some slightly underhand methods in the battle for converts, including the pirating of interesting symbols, ideas and holidays from their rivals. The Seven Deadly Sins were copied wholesale from the arch-rival sect of Mithraism (*see* p.88).

Dedicated to keeping the canon up to date, the instructive Deadly Sins' Homepage    www.deadlysins.com/ reveals that in modern times the Sins have gone undercover to infiltrate children's minds—for example as the dwarfs in Walt Disney's Snow White:

*Seven shrunken men shacked up in a secluded forest cabin, hiding a virginal teenage runaway. Seven tortured forms shouldering their demonic tools as they march into the hellish bowels of the earth, singing as they go....*

Adam Shannon, the monk in charge of the page, also offers the best explanation for an insidious vehicle that launched the Deadly Sins straight into the heart of Middle America's living rooms: the 1965–67 sitcom, *Gilligan's Island*. Gilligan and six other castaways, trapped on a Pacific island, seem to be as harmless and oafish as

any characters on American TV, and yet the show turns out to be:

*a Sartre-like nether-world in which the characters represent the Seven Deadly Sins, forced in the days after Armageddon (in the form of the Flood) to live in unceasing torment with each other. The viewers witness the characters' eternal damnation through Gilligan, a name derived from the Scottish 'gillie', a hunting or fishing guide.*

Not only hidden in Disney and on *Gilligan's Island*, the Sins are openly present in such divers entertainments as Kurt Weill's musical on the Deadlies and the dark and gloomy serial killer thriller, *Seven*. It's a shame there are only four Spice Girls. The truth is, thanks to modern technology, the Deadlies have become bigger and brasher than ever and pop culture openly encourages every last one of them.

**Pride/Vanity**: under the Sun.

Preceding every fall stands Pride, the mother of sins. Even the most holy, virginal and pious saints have occasionally tripped over the thin line between righteousness and self-righteousness. What has changed in recent years, is that Pride has become socially acceptable, especially in the

United States, where 'We're Number One!' and 'Don't dis me!' are heard on every side; Barney the Dinosaur, telling small children that they're all 'special' instead of the good old-fashioned 'seen and not heard', is doing Beezelbub's job (you always wondered who was zipped up in that purple costume). Sport shoe designers, plastic surgeons and Madonna are doing the rest.

about, or say they do, when indulging in something sinfully delicious.

**Greed/Covetousness**: under the sign of Mercury.

Hell's special ambassador to England, Mammon, is in charge of Avarice, and throughout history it is a traditional banana peel on which Anglo-Saxons from either side of the Atlantic have slipped. Now the whole world is caught up in the

## Christian hell, invented by a celibate clergy, has always afforded the best in kinky sadomasochistic punishments

**Envy**: under the sign of the Moon.

The reverse of pride: the sorry state of not possessing designer sport-shoes, silicone breasts or Madonna. Modern capitalism is fueled on envy; it is the key behind every advertisement. No envy, no greed. Bitchily resenting other people's success and happiness has come out of the closet, especially in the New Britain.

**Gluttony**: under the sign of Jupiter.

Ambition was the original Mithraic sin, but, when it changed sides and became a virtue, Gluttony was summoned to take its place. The modern cult of emaciation makes this the one Deadly Sin that people still feel guilty

frenzy, and the most successful sinners have become more obscenely rich than ever. But rather than despise them as robber barons, society courts them as heroic capitalists.

**Lust**: under the sign of Venus.

The opportunities for enjoying this fave Deadly Sin continue to grow exponentially thanks to birth control, Viagra, and simply more people around to lust after. It has other advantages as well: Christian hell, invented by a celibate clergy, has always afforded the best in kinky sadomasochistic punishments, although the very worst are always reserved for erring monks and nuns.

**Wrath**: under the sign of Mars.

Wrath has always been one of the nastier sins, and remains so in spite of the dictums of mental health experts encouraging folks to blow off steam and let it all hang out. Wrath is the one Deadly Sin most likely to hurt other people, especially when put into a cocktail shaker with another sin: Wrath plus Envy equals armed robbery; Wrath plus Lust equals rape; Wrath plus Gluttony equals stealing candy from babies, or at least gross table manners.

**Sloth**: under the sign of Saturn.

This is one we all long for, but rarely get to enjoy; every passing decade would seem to make sloth easier to achieve, with the invention of new labour-saving devices. Only who has the leisure to enjoy sloth? The couch potatoes who manage to achieve genuine laziness all seem willing to pay the high cost of watching TV all day. Note that originally this sin was *Accidia*—spiritual sloth, a lack of concern about the Big Issues. Eventually the Church found that almost everyone was guilty of this one, so they gave in to pressure from the business interests and changed it to something a little more practical.

If you want to take a road less travelled, you'll get to Hell if you

♣ draw the Dead Man's Hand. This is two pair, aces and eights. That's what Wild Bill Hickok was holding when Jack McCall shot him with a Colt.45 in Deadwood, South Dakota in 1876. He still had the cards in a death grip when they carried him out the door. The fifth card was the four of clubs, the unluckiest card in the deck—poker players call it the 'Devil's bedposts'.

♣ be first to be buried in a new graveyard: traditionally the first customer is carried off by the Devil, so in places they would bury a dog first.

♣ get the Pope to send you. Sigismundo Malatesta, the 15th-century ruler of Rimini who spent his career attacking and bullying the Papal States, and allegedly raping his own son and daughter, was so awful that Pope Pius II took the unusual measure of canonizing him to Hell, while he was still alive: as far as we know he is Hell's only 'saint'. ❀

## Points of Entry

Several entrances have been used by visitors since ancient times: the cave of Taenerus in the southern Peloponnese, Lake Avernus on the bay of Naples, the Cave of Cehennem on the Silician coast, Mount Etna or Lake Pergusa in Sicily ('sailing to Sicily' means going to hell) and icy, fuming Iceland, in the extreme north (the north is the Devil's particular direction, and the reason why the north side of a churchyard was unconsecrated ground, good only for suicides). Paris had an entrance back when it was still a naughty, fun medieval city ruled by the lusty demon Belphegor.

In short, Hell is **a big place**. Jesus once forced the Devil to measure it, and he came up with a figure of 100,000 miles in each direction. Galileo, for a facetious student project, calculated that Hell lies precisely 405 12/22 miles beneath the earth's surface. But it also appears that Hell's frontiers fluctuate. Not too long ago, God caught the devil moving the fence a few feet and He said:

'Hey, you can't do that!'.

'Who says I can't?' replied the devil.

'Why, I'll take you to court, and you'll see!' said God.

'Oh? And who do You have up in Heaven to represent You?'

# infernal Geography

Going to Hell is a lot like **air travel**. If you want to go to Ljubljana or Curitiba or Tientsin, any travel agent can book you a ticket, even if neither of you could find the place on a map. Despite the years of research that have gone into this book, we still aren't sure ourselves where Hell is located. Nevertheless, we are certain we'll have no trouble reaching it.

For many Christians, this isn't enough. It was Sister Mary Thomas, back in Sunday school, who first brought up the issue. Sister Mary Thomas could be obscure at times, especially when dealing with the higher mysteries, but she did leave a definite impression, one that coincided with the common opinion of poets, philosophers and theologians since the time of Homer and Hesiod. Heaven was Up Above our world (way over the North Pole, we thought). Hell was Down Below, at the bottom of the universe (and what was underneath that, we wondered?). It seemed plausible to assume that Limbo and Purgatory were off on the left and right ends of the universe, making the kind of neat, symmetrical cosmos

Catholics have always favoured. None of us would ever imagine that Hell could be inside the earth, since we had all seen James Mason take Arlene Dahl and Pat Boone down there in *Journey to the Center of the Earth* at the Granada Theater. They found monsters, sure, but no devils. Case closed. The first Soviet cosmonaut came home and reported that he had been among the stars, and had seen no God and no Heaven there. Ever since, those pesky scientists have been pointing their rocket ships and their telescopes in every direction. They have completed the work that Jules Verne started, wrecking that pretty old cosmos and forcing us to start designing a new one. Don't ask any modern Catholic where Hell is; they're not in the mood for silly questions. However, many fundamentalist Protestants are still looking.

The fundamentalists may disdain scientific opinions, but some of them never stop trying to adapt the teachings of the Bible to the latest news from the observatories. They have come up with a few possible new locations for Hell:

*TARTARUS*

Orbita Saturni

Orbita Jovis

Orbita Martis

Orbita Telluris

Orbita Veneris

Orbita Mercurii

**Venus**. David Webber and Noah Hutchings, of the Southwest Radio Church in Oklahoma City, think Venus might just be the place. And it makes sense. As the morning star, Venus has long been identified with Lucifer, the light-bringer; it was a star of evil portent long before the Devil was invented. The scientists say that the planet is an ocean of boiling hot methane gas, with a temperature of about 800°F on the surface, and Webber and Hutchings note that even NASA has had to resort to Biblical terminology to describe it. Venus is completely covered with clouds, and nobody has ever seen what it's like down on the surface, so they may be right.

**Black Holes**. These chilling, all-devouring monsters provide a perfect Space Age update of the medieval image of the Mouth of Hell. No matter can escape one if it gets too close, but spiritual beings like devils might have no problem.

**Dwarf Stars**. Some scientists argued that these hot, dense stars can theoretically burn on forever. Radio preachers cite this as evidence that 'the Lake of Fire has been prepared, and is now ready'.

**An Einstein-Rosen Bridge**. Also known as 'wormholes', these strange artefacts of quantum theory, related to black holes, are theoretical connections between separate universes where time as we know it does not exist. Webber and Hutchings are on to this one too; they may have learned about them from Star Trek, where wormholes feature in several episodes. The preachers say that if you get stuck in one of these you're in for a relative eternity of horrible punishment, and they refer wormhole-scoffers to Isaiah 66:24: 'The Worm shall not die, neither shall the fire be quenched.'

**A Parallel Universe**. Many physicists today subscribe to the 'Many Worlds' interpretation of quantum theory, which states that all conceivable universes not only can, but must exist. The mathematics make it necessary, they say, though how to apply the equations to reality is still something of a problem. If it's true, then one of these universes has to be a Christian Heaven, and another a Christian Hell. Try arguing against that one; you will fail. The Devil undoubtedly knows how to navigate his way around all these universes, and there's no reason why he can't just pop into your bedroom, like Mr. Mxyptlyk from the Fifth Dimension in the old Superman comics, any time he feels like it. ♠

*Many of us go through Hell all the time without giving much consideration to what it would be like to park and get out of the car. But some infernal savvy may well pay off when you pull into the last Dead End.*

## Your Host:
## Not Such A Bad Dude Once You Get To Know Him

eternal practicalities

*I had no ail,
until popular belief
gave it to me*

the Devil

This quote comes from one of the most revealing in-depth interviews the Old Enemy has ever accorded. Paris has always been one of his favourite towns, especially in the spring, and he told all in 1825 to a Parisian named Collin de Plancey, who wrote it down in *Le Diable Peint par Lui-même*. Sympathy for the Devil becomes all too easy when you hear the story from his point of view. He told de Plancey that he wasn't bad-looking when he started his career in evil, but God decreed that whatever wounds and deformities he suffered along the way, he had to keep. This included not only the real injuries, such as an eternally sore nose ever since St Dunstan had pulled it with red hot tongs some thousand years ago, but all the blows and barbs of slander and character assassination the human race can dream up. Back in 1825, one of the great secrets of the universe was revealed—whatever we say about the Devil becomes true. Step on a crack, you break the Devil's back.

Mothers and nurses gave him his horns, as they spun tales by the fireside to frighten their wayward children. His skin grew rough and scaly from so many millennia down in the fire and smoke, and his bones are woefully bent out of shape from having to squeeze through all those keyholes in the fairy stories. Every time some exorcist bashes a possessed soul around the ears to drive out a demon, the Devil feels it.

# eternity

Hell's Proprietor seems to be of Persian origin, a creation of the drastic division between good and evil begun by the Zoroastrians (*see* p.78). The Jews evidently picked up some of these ideas after their Babylonian Captivity, though their original Satan did not start out as an embodiment of Evil but rather a being charged by Yahweh with inflicting sufferings—as he did to Job. When the Old Testament was first translated into Greek, in Hellenistic Egypt, the translators rendered Satan as Diabolos, and both names have been pretty much interchangeable ever since.

For making him the particular adversary of mankind, we can thank the early Christians, though he does not really have a big role in the New Testament (*see* p.92). Once their new, high-octane Devil was established, the only thing lacking was the gory details. No one did more to create

the image of the Devil we know than the early Christian hermits of Egypt, the 'fathers of the desert'. These spiritual athletes, alone in the waste lands with their neuroses, were pestered constantly by devils as they wrestled with their burdens of guilt and sin. In the *Life of St Anthony* and Jerome's *Life of St Hilary* we first hear of goat horns and cloven feet, of a devil who can assume any shape or form from asses to angels, who can inhabit the bodies of men, women or even animals (one of the first recorded exorcisms was apparently performed on a camel).

He's a big fellow, about eight feet tall in Hell according to de Plancey, though he doesn't often frighten people by appearing that way on Earth. In fact, these days when he goes walking he usually leaves his horns and tail hanging on a hook in the closet.

Caesarius of Heisterbach, the 13th-century author of *The Dialogue of Miracles*, explains that God isn't the only one who can perform miracles. Caesarius cites cases where the Devil has changed himself into horses, bears, dragons, cats, cows, toads, or whatever else serves his purposes. In the southern States, where he spends a lot of his time, he's most often seen as a rabbit, a terrapin, a housefly, a yellow dog or a black billy goat. Arkansas folklorist Vance Packard met an old man in the Ozarks who once saw the Devil walking in the snow near the Missouri line:

*When I questioned him about the Devil's appearance, he described an ordinary countryman—blue over-alls, slouch hat, skinny face, long hair, shotgun on shoulder, and so on. 'He just looked like any common ordinary feller', said the old man wonderingly. I pondered this for a while. 'But how did you know it was the Devil?' I asked. The old man looked fearfully around, then leaned toward me and whispered: 'He didn't throw no shadder! He didn't leave no tracks!'*

But even if you meet your Devil on a paved street, on a cloudy day, you needn't be deceived if you look closely. Caesarius of Heisterbach points out that by divine injunction the Devil can never make his disguise perfect. There's always one little flaw, and if it isn't a cloven foot you might find it situated in the region of the buttocks. Devils don't have bottoms; maybe it's a little joke on God's part. Everyone in the Middle Ages knew this. In almost any old woodcut or fresco where this part of a devil is exposed, you'll notice that instead of a bottom there is another face.

It isn't a very nice face, and, for what comes out of it, it might as well have stayed a bum. For all the hell-raising sermonizing of the Middle Ages, there was also a constant and very healthy tendency to reduce the great terror to the level of children's bathroom humour. In Arnoul

> Devils don't have bottoms; maybe it's a little joke on God's part. Everyone in the Middle Ages knew this.

Greban's 14th-century passion play, the Devil has, in addition to the usual things one would expect to find in such a place, no less than 20,000 friars up his behind.

Devils in Western art often have faces on their kneecaps too, hence an old British expression, 'as the Devil said to his knee-buckles...'

Once you've discovered the Devil, you may want to get rid of him. Don't confuse him with vampires—crosses and garlic have no effect at all. Calling on the name of Our Lord Jesus Christ will usually suffice to make him leave the room (though

this has the same effect on other human beings). Some herbs have built reputations as Devil-repellents, notably asafoetida, which the Germans have charmingly called *Teufelsdrockh*. He has a strange hatred of salt too, and they say he can be baffled with fern seed (of course, there's no such thing as fern seed). Women, who are worse than devils, can be of much assistance; probably every nation in Europe has a folk-tale about some poor soul who gets into trouble with the Devil and is saved by a horrible shrewish wife. Perusing the fairytales, we might even feel sorry for the fellow. He always loses. He goes to all the trouble of building those bridges and towers, and some simple Christian always cheats him out of the fruits of his labour. And quite often he gets a good hiding on top of it. Another very widespread folk-tale motif is the story (like, for example, Brueder Lustig in the Grimm tales) of the mustered-out soldier who bargains his soul for a magic sack, one that immediately produces anything he wishes to be in it. Of course, when the Devil comes for his due, Brueder Lustig wishes him into the sack and then beats him black and blue until he promises to go away.

The cross-cultural similarities in Devil stories can be downright uncanny. One of Italo Calvino's Italian folktales concerns a strong young lad named Fourteen (because he was a fourteenth son; twice as good as a seventh son) who goes down to Hell and robs the Devil of his gold, kills fourteen of his best demons, takes the Devil himself back home and ties him to the kitchen table leg. Now, down in Dixie there was an African-American tale of a similar fellow named Big Sixteen (because that was his shoe size), who digs a hole down to Hell, where he whacks the Devil over the head with a sledge hammer and kills him dead. When Big Sixteen dies, Heaven is afraid to take him so he goes down to Hell again. This time he meets the Devil's widow, who gives him a hot coal and tells him to 'g'wan off and start a Hell of yo' own'.

So why are Devil stories so alike? The only possible explanation is: they all must be true.

We call him Old Horny, Old Hairy, Black Bogey, Lusty Dick, the Dickens, Old Nick, Old Scratch, Old Iniquity, along with careful euphemisms like the 'Good Fellow' or 'Gentleman Jack'. Every nation and age has contributed its own—too many for anyone to remember. H. L. Mencken recorded a list of archaic devil names from the 1830s remarking 'some certainly deserve revival, if only for use as objurgations': Cocabelto, Kellicocam, Motubizanto, Arraba, Lacahabarratu, Ju, Oguerracatam, Buzache, Knockadwe among them.

'Pleased to meet you…won't you guess my name?' One of the Devil's more endearing traits is his fondness for riddles. God's laws are plain and straightforward, and a little boring at times, and anything that involves complexity and paradox is much more likely to delight a diabolical mind. This goes for the visual arts too, and cultures from Celtic Europe to Southeast Asia would draw intricate patterns or weave patterns of knots to catch out demons, who would become so involved with following the complexities of the pattern that they would forget the deviltry they were sent to do.

He is always likely to pop up asking difficult questions, and you had better know the answers if you don't want to get carried off. The innocence of a child is usually enough to defeat him, as in the famous old ballad found across the English-speaking world (this one's from Nova Scotia):

*What is higher than a tree,*
*what is deeper than the sea?*
*Cried the false knight*
*to the child on the road.*
*'Heaven's higher than a tree;*
*Hell is deeper than the sea,'*
*Cried the pretty little child*
*only seven years old.*

One riddle the Devil doesn't really appreciate is 'What is the distance between Heaven and Hell?' He knows the answer only too well: one step. 🌿

# climate

Who says Hell's so hot? Prophets and theologians from the sunny climes of the Middle East and the Mediterranean, that's who. Folklore scholars have long noted that peoples in hot climates invent hot Hells, while in more northerly latitudes folks imagine icy frozen ones. Like London or Washington DC, Hell has always had to endure slanderous remarks about its weather from people who've never even been there.

The truth is that Hell contains a vast range of climates. Buddhists say there are eight hot hells and eight cold hells, and even some early Christian traditions found some frigid chambers down below. There is plenty of heat in the various circles of Dante's *Inferno*, though the great, numb Devil is frozen solid in a pit of ice, which he keeps cool by absent-mindedly beating his vast leathery wings.

Scientific opinions on this subject would be difficult, though hardly impossible. Recently a physics professor gave his class an exam with the question *Is Hell endothermic or exothermic?* A wide range of answers was noted, most of them of little scientific merit. A few were rather abrupt, and betrayed some irritation, though one student managed a close analysis of the problem, using Boyle's Law, and came to this conclusion:

> *So if Hell is expanding at a slower rate than the rate at which souls are entering it, then the temperature and pressure will increase until all Hell breaks loose.*
>
> *Of course, if Hell is expanding at a rate faster than the increase of souls in Hell, then the temperature and pressure will necessarily drop until Hell freezes over.*

## Calling Home ( 666–)

Since the boisterous renaissance of spiritualism in the last century, people have been crazy for any news from the great Out Yonder. Mediums, hypnotists and investigators of near-death experiences get regular reports from various astral planes, from all sorts of purgatories, from just about anywhere, in fact, but not from Hell. The gates there appear to be shut tight, and an essential part of the whole experience seems to be enjoying a total break from the stressful world you left behind—rather like the Club Med.

Modern technology breaks down all the old barriers, they say, and in recent years there has been a great increase in the phenomenon of phone calls from the departed. Thomas Edison, whose parents were spiritualists, spent time working on a machine especially designed for contacting the dead, without success, but these days the dead themselves are constantly finding new ways to get inside the lines. Often they try to warn the person they call of some impending disaster, or tell them where they hid the dough—as if this were some old *Twilight Zone* episode—though some people report getting calls from dead people who are total strangers. Connections are usually bad, and the voices tend to fade away. Most of these calls happen a day or two after the death of the individual—the Devil, like the police, allows you just one call and that's it (details can be found in a book called *Phone Calls From the Dead*, by D. Scott Rogo and Raymond Bayless, 1979).

## Post Offices

The mail service in Hell is even worse than the Italian post. Only one letter has made it through from the Devil, kept in the cathedral of Agrigento in Sicily, written in a wild, incomprehensible script shot through with magical symbols. Addressed to a local virgin, it is a pathetic attempt to seduce her soul away, offering her all the treasures of the world in exchange for her virtue; the girl in question indignantly

the Devil,
like the police,
allows you one call
and that's it

carnal practicalities

turned it over to her priest (another city in Sicily, Messina, had a special letter direct from the Virgin, which has balanced things out on the big island).

Other realms of punishment tend to be a little more liberal about communications. In the gloomy old church of St-Eustache, just around the corner from where Les Halles used to be in Paris, there is an old wooden box with a slot in the top in one of the chapels off the right aisle; on it is a card bearing a note in a crabbed hand, which reads *Messages for Souls in Purgatory*. The souls in Purgatory occasionally reply: in Rome, you can peruse their missives in the Museo del Purgatorio, housed in the church of the Sacro Cuore del Suffragio, near Castel Sant' Angelo, in the prayer books and fabrics authenticated with scorched handmarks.

There are, however, messages direct from the devil on line: Charles Manson has composed a number of essays on the subject of true evil, at *http://members.aa.net/~wdevil/* or you can enjoy the lyrics of his songs ('People say I'm no good') at *http://www.atwa.com/index.htm*.

## Hell's Kitchen: Food and Drink

You weren't expecting any, were you? If you're staying for good, the closest you'll probably come is a bottle of beer on a string just out of reach, one that descends ever so slowly, and when you finally can grab it you find it's empty, like all the other ones (as in Lord Dunsany's play, *The Glittering Gate*). For those planning just a short stay, though, it's important not to touch a bite, or take a sip. If you don't believe us, take it from the Celts, the Lapps, the Jews, the New Caledonians, the Greeks, the Cherokee, the Maori, the Kwakiutl and dozens of other peoples around the globe. Folklore and mythology of all times and places agree: once you have supped with the denizens of the underworld, you're one of them, and you'll never get out.

Persephone's abduction by Hades provides the best-known example. One pomegranate seed accepted in a weak moment was all it took (some say it was seven; seven is a very important number in Hell). What was Hades doing with pomegranates? No one has come up with a convincing explanation for that one; pomegranates are usually associated with

**Even in this world, wherever beer goes creatures from Hell are seldom far behind**

fertility; some scholars have claimed that the apple in the Garden of Eden was really a pomegranate.

In the national epic of Finland, the *Kalevala*, where battles are fought not with swords, but with magic words and runes, the hero Väinämöinen continually gets himself in the strangest fixes. To win his true love, a maiden who sits on a rainbow weaving golden nets, he has to make a boat from the splinters of a spindle. Väinämöinen nearly manages it with a magic song, but there are three words in the song he doesn't know, and he has to go to Tuonela, the abode of the dead, to get them. The dead greet him at the gate with a big seidel of beer, but Väinämöinen, being well-schooled in these matters, has sense enough to decline. He gets out, though he never does learn the magic words, and never gets the girl.

Beer may not go especially well with pomegranates, but, ever since Gilgamesh chatted up the other-world barmaid Siduri on his way to find the secret of immortality, it has always been the elixir of choice in the lands beyond. Even in this world, wherever beer goes creatures from Hell are seldom far behind. The great ethnologist Leo Frobenius (*Und Afrika Sprach...*, Berlin, 1912) visited the people of the Bori and Asama, two animistic religions of central Africa which forbade the drinking of beer. Frobenius, who brought some along for clinical studies, wrote that:

> 'When a follower of Bori takes beer, the alledjenu *[black spirit]* swoops down upon him like the wind. His eyes are filled with darkness. Then the alledjenu *has seized him; the man falls as if dead.'*

Other ethnologists have noted similar phenomena among men in certain tribes of the English-speaking world.

These know no cure for possession by *alledjenu*, but the Bori have an elaborate ritual to cure their unfortunates. A musician, playing the *goye*, or else a violin or guitar, plays the chords and melodies that correspond in music-language to the names of the different *alledjenus*. When exactly the correct music is found, the spirit returns to the body and causes another fit. The *adjingi*, or doctor, who has already treated the victim with the broth and smoke of the proper herbs, now knows which demon he is dealing with, and proceeds to administer just the right medicines, sitting with the victim for seven days 'to the sound of the violin and the beating of the calabash'.

After the *alledjenu* has departed, a festival is arranged with sacred dancing and the sacrifice of a white ram. Sometimes the dancing 'degenerates into triviality and amusement', but if things go right white spirits, or *fari-farus*, take hold of some people with a prophetic trance.

The Muslims have it all their own way in that part of Africa now, and all the old Bori habits are frowned upon by the police. Which is a pity, for no one on earth has ever got more out of a glass of beer.

# entertainment

The Devil, as everybody knows, is a mean fiddler. In the folktales he gets higher marks for technical virtuosity than for nuance, playing a lightning-fast infernal jig that bewitches folks and keeps them dancing until they drop. In Tibet and as far south as Sri Lanka, a survival of old shamanistic religions called the 'devil dance' would happen whenever a demon got into somebody. The possessed person would simply have to dance in a frenzied manner until the demon got tired and left. As late as a century ago in the south Italian province of Taranto, people bitten by a certain poisonous spider would call over musicians and dance for days until

eternal practicalities

HELL'S BELLBOTTOMS

**21**

the evil spirit of the poison worked itself out. The music they played made its way to the dance halls of Naples and became the *tarantella* (hence also tarantulas).

You might suspect that the Devil has got himself one hell of a band down below. Paganini and Liszt were both suspected of making private deals with him (for the record, their contemporary Hector Berlioz circulated the only known score for a chorus of devils, in their own private language no less, in his *Damnation de Faust*), and, if by some quirk of fate Gene Krupa or Jimi Hendrix ended up in Heaven, we can be sure Old Scratch would be around in a minute to see if God would sell him their contracts. For any soul with a large daily rhythm requirement, Hell could be even better than dying and going to 52nd Street.

If it's Stephane Grappelli you want, you'll find him up on a cloud playing *C'est Si Bon* with the angels, but in Hell you can get the proprietor himself duelling fiddles in 11/16 time with Stuff Smith or Joe Venuti. Lady Day and Lester Young are reunited forever where the smoke swirls and the lights are low, while Mr. Tatum, Mr. Beiderbecke and Mr. Parker can forget earthly spectres like money,

bus trips, sobriety and the police and concentrate on the music. Down here even Sinatra sounds good.

If Hell is a Church of England Hell, Louis Armstrong will definitely be in it. Back in the 1940s, when his band was playing a special concert with King George and the royal family in attendance, Louis announced that the next number would be *I'll Be Glad When You're Dead You Rascal You*. Then he gave the King a wink and said 'This one's for you, Rex.'

## If Hell is a Church of England Hell, Louis Armstrong will definitely be in it

**The bad news is**...tastes and fashions change, and if music is in a hell of a state up here you can imagine what it must be like down there. Lately, there have been disturbing indications that many top hits on the infernal charts come from Norway.

Most people would agree that Norway is the most boring country in the world, and young Norwegian Beavises and Buttheads aren't taking it lying down. Along with their friends in other Scandinavian countries, they have taken heavy metal music over from the British and Americans and made it their own. Metal lyrics, when they can be understood, show an obsession with the things of the Devil, and the music is closely tied to Scandinavian neo-pagan and sometimes neo-Nazi groups. It's an anarchistic rebellion, couched in the terms of Satanism, against what they call the 'giant, cancerous, duty-bound social organism' of modern life.

Serious metal has serious apologists—try *www.evilmusic.com*. Current trends in Scandinavian metal seem to be divided into two major categories. Aficionados define **Death Metal** as 'the science of incorporating nihilistic brutality and frustrated anger of modern life into an art form

of sound'. Hot groups include Slayer, Morbid Angel, Pestilence, Sepultura and the ever-popular Kataklysm.

**Black Metal**, unlike Death Metal, is said to 'foment chaos and disturbances in your mind'. Topping the Black Metal charts is Mayhem, with its legendary lead singer Dead (unfortunately, he is). When Dead was still around they had a number of hits, including *Chainsaw Gutsfuck*, *Deathcrush* and the melodious *Pure Fucking Armageddon*. Dead got that way at the hands of Count Grishnackh, lead singer of rival band Barzum; they gave him 21 years.

There is definitely method in the metal madness. Scandinavian metalheads have read all the pop science books, are fond of talking about finding new patterns in Chaos and like to pose their arguments in terms from computer terminology:

> '...control builds a structure but Satan encodes himself in the structure. Soon the structure begins to decay, as the Lord of Obscurity introduces his virus of ambiguity.'

On the whole, the phenomenon doesn't seem too far removed from John Cage or Pierre Boulez. You can't whistle it; you can't dance to it.

The Hell with it.

eternal predicaments

# holidays

Hell never closes, although people sometimes get time off for the good deeds they performed while alive. Even Judas Iscariot, who had once given a cloak to a leper in Joppa, gets a furlough at least once a year. St Brandon met his soul on an iceberg, and Matthew Arnold put the incident in a poem.

In Mexico, all the dead get to return home on All Soul's Day (1 November). The Day of the Dead, *Dia de los Muertos*, begins with a candle-light procession to the cemetery, in which friends and relatives bring food and flowers, have a meal, and decorate an altar to the deceased, with their photo and all their favourite things. There's a lot of horsing around with the *calaca*, the Grim Reaper, an image straight from the medieval Dance of Death. But

before you reach the skeleton-prancing stage, be aware of another holiday (and it's not Hallowe'en).

*Did you hear about the dyslexic devil-worshipper who sold his soul to Santa?*

It's no joke. Devotees of the Christmas cult would do well to ask themselves, just who is this St Nicholas fellow, anyway? Nicholas of Myra is a shadowy character, who in medieval times became the patron saint of thieves and pawnbrokers. You can see his body in Bari, Italy still oozing a miraculous liquid that is collected in phials to help people avoid bad luck and win the lottery.

But every important saint is really a mixture of many old stories and beliefs. Jeffrey Burton Russell, author of *Lucifer: The Devil in the Middle Ages*, finds some intriguing parallels with the Devil of north European folklore:

In addition to his association with the north and reindeer, the Devil can wear red fur; he is covered with soot and goes down chimneys in the guise of Black Jack or the Black Man; he carries a large sack into which he pops sins or sinners (including naughty children); he carries a stick or cane to thrash the guilty (the origin of the candy cane); he flies through the air with the help of animals; food and wine are left out for him as a bribe.

The Devil's nickname (!) of Old Nick derives directly from St Nicholas who was often associated with fertility cults, hence with fruit, nuts, and fruitcake.

The evidence seems conclusive. The Devil can assume many shapes, but perhaps he isn't as clever as people think. It took him nearly 2000 years to perfect a disguise that would be the perfect vehicle for Temptation.

## Handle with Care

As Hell is only officially open to permanent residents, tourist information is cleverly disguised under a different name. Think of Satanist groups as cultural embassies, a way to learn a little about what awaits Downside—rather like the *Alliance Française* only with incantations instead of conjugations.

Though **Satanism** is essentially a modern phenomenon, accusations of devil worship have been around as long as there have been priests. The early Christian sects accused each other of doing it. Then for centuries, with straight faces and fingers crossed behind their backs, the priests swore the Muslims did it. Wherever in Europe people attempted to hold on to their old religions, especially in the Celtic lands, they, of course, had to be Satanists too.

In the witchcraft scares of the Middle Ages, prosecutors always brought the Devil into it, and under torture the 'witches' were only too glad to fill in the demonic details. True believers didn't start to gather until the 19th century, that great age of progress that also brought in Gothic novels, seances and Edgar Allan Poe. According to Russell Hope Robbins, in his *Encyclopedia of Demonology and Witchcraft*, the Satanic mass was also a literary creation. The hysterically embellished accounts of the witch-hunters and inquisitors certainly helped in establishing the framework, but it was essentially modern souls who created the concept as we know it today. One of the earliest and most influential was none other than the **Marquis de Sade**. In his novel *Justine*, de Sade provides an example of a Satanic mass that helped define the genre. Young virtuous Justine gets tricked into participating in the affair by libertine monks, who use her for the altar, and then take turns having their way with her.

As for the term **'Black Mass'**, this does not occur in print until over a hundred years later, in 1896. In our own century, the flame was kept alive by the Great Beast himself, Aleister Crowley. His writings contain all sorts of diabolical mumbo-jumbo, and hints of human sacrifices, but from the evidence it seems that the greatest concern of Crowley and his followers was having lots of kinky sex in an exotic atmosphere of candles and costumes. The orgies Crowley hosted at his home in Cefalù, Sicily, became so notorious in the 1920s that

Mussolini himself ordered him expelled from Italy.

In our sordid times, allegations of Satanism have grown into a thriving cottage industry. The most recent, and most serious Satanist, scare began in America in the 1980s. Though helped along by the supermarket tabloids, the fundamentalist preachers and television, the spark that set this one off was a book called *Satan's Underground*, a detailed account of a woman's childhood traumas at the hands of Satanist parents that was eventually exposed as a fraud. Through this, Satanism became wound up in the bizarre contemporary phenomenon of 'recovered memories'. In an eerie reprise of

was hatched. Soon, a self-proclaimed 'crime expert' from Chicago named Simandel was touring the country giving seminars to police in how to deal with Satanic crimes, the 'crime of the nineties', and a national police association estimated that 1.4 million Americans were involved in Satanic worship. One earnest cop in Indiana wrote:

> *When a police officer finds himself confronting the Prince of Darkness or his legions, he had better have the 'scourge of Satan' [the Bible] at his side as well as all the spiritual aids and weapons he can muster. In the war against Satanic crimes, Christian officers are the ones best prepared to be the spearhead.*

## Think of Satanist groups as cultural embassies— rather like *Alliance Française* only with incantations instead of conjugations

the long-ago witch trials, trained and certified psychologists encouraged unbalanced 'victims' to 'recover' supposedly suppressed details of dark rituals and abuse from their childhoods. The power of suggestion proved stronger even than the Devil's, and a full-blown paranoia

For another artefact of the current madness, you can send to Hearthstone Publishing in Oklahoma City for a book called *14 Things Witches Hope Parents Never Find Out*, which explains how witches recruit children, and how to distinguish good witches from bad ones.

The alarm spread to Britain too, as did the 'recovered memories' scam, most sensationally in a case of alleged Satanic child abuse on the Orkney Islands; an inquiry later attributed this to over-zealous social workers who suggested all the details of the affair to the children, exactly as the inquisitors used to do in the witch hunts. Copycat cases began appearing all over Britain—84 of them, all were proved bogus. Nevertheless the damage was done. The tabloids had a field day, while the Vehicle Licensing Centre decided to stop giving out the number 666. In 1993, Princess Diana's brother, Earl Spencer, made his maiden speech in the House of Lords on the subject of Satanism in Harlestone Woods.

In fact Britain and Europe undoubtedly have more serious Satanic groups then America. Turin, Italy, where the devil-worshippers meet in the city sewers, may be the world capital of this business, with Paris and London close behind. And plenty of young scruffy Norwegians, influenced by neo-pagan ideologies and metal music, are winding up in jail for burning down churches.

As for America, it may be worth noting that the only man currently in jail for 'Satanist crimes' is a former official of the Republican Party in Washington state. It's probably more significant that he too seems to be an innocent victim of 'recovered memories', but nevertheless the ideological kinship between contemporary Satanism and the northern and west coast strains of conservatism is strong. Both are socially libertarian, with a belief in man's fundamental inequality, and many conservatives tend to be enthusiastically, though secretly, perverse.

The reigning celebrity of American Satanism is Anton LaVey, a former carnival organist and police photographer who founded the Church of Satan in San Francisco, and wrote an extremely popular book called *The Satanists' Bible*. LaVey's game is a sort of Californian worship of the Self run rampant. His policies for this world seem to be lifted straight from Ayn Rand; LaVey's Bible proclaims 'Death to the weaklings, wealth to the Strong!' and in it you will find nothing more subversive than a proposal for cloning humans to provide slaves for Satanist masters, along with a good helping of adolescent atheism:

*I gaze into the glassy eye of your fearsome Jehovah and pluck him by the beard; I uplift a broadaxe and split open his worm-eaten skull.*

The FBI undoubtedly keeps an eye on LaVey's followers, though there aren't many. Another California Satanist group is the Process Church of Robert de Grimston, which has made a saint of the serial killer 'Son of Sam'. Beyond these, such 'Satanism' as exists in the US seems to be relatively harmless play-acting on the part of middle-aged sex perverts or spaced-out metalhead teens. Or else it could be a cover used by genuine villains; there has been evidence that some drug gangs employ Satanist rituals and murders as part of a terror tactic to keep their soldiers in line.

For the sunny side of Satanism, you might consult the Satanic Network at *www. satannet.com*; or the '600 Club' at *www.the600club.com*; the name seems to suggest they demand less in contributions than Pat Robertson's 700 Club.

Incidentally Christian investigators and publications in the US have done more than anyone to expose the fantasies of the Satanist hysteria; there is a good Christian website debunking Satanism at *www.answers. org/Satan*. And for the most lucid information anywhere on the internet concerning modern Satanism (and indeed many other subjects),

just dial up the remarkable site run by the Sheriff's Office of Anderson County in South Carolina: *www.carol.net/acsa/satan*.

Of course, there are a few real devil-worshippers in the world, but most of them live in Kurdistan. The Yezidis, or **'Peacock Angel Cult'**, have been around at least since the 12th century. Their belief is a kind of Manichaeanism turned inside-out. Satan, or Malak Ta'us, the 'Peacock Angel', did rebel against God, and was cast into Hell, but he was so sorry for it that his tears of remorse put out all the infernal fires. Now a good angel again, he does rule over this world, with the help of six other powerful angels, while the original God is far away and does not concern himself too much in our affairs.

Yezidis are mostly country people in remote places. These days they come under strong pressure from Muslim fundamentalists, but you might still find one of their strange serpent-bearing processions in a village of Turkey or Iraq.

So there you are; if you want to go to Hell, just look at the sort of company you will be keeping. ۞

## Hell on Wheels

The very idea of straddling a big throbbing machine, the speed, noise, freedom, the leather kit...the minute technological progress on earth permitted the invention of the motorcycle, the Devil retired his black goat for the new form of locomotion. In 1948, he granted his favourite minions in San Bernardino the chance to ride Hogs around California scaring the bejesus out of everybody. And fifty years on, they're still at it; Hell's Angels now count 1,600 members, in every continent, not including fledgling Angels in probationary bands (the Grim Reapers, Satan's Choice, Para Dice Riders). Spokesmen for the club claim they are a harmless bunch of guys, devoted to the motorcycle culture; police demur, and say they are an organized crime syndicate doing the Devil's work, distributing drugs, receiving kickbacks from strip joints, and murdering rivals.

But this is the 1990s, and Hell Inc. has recently authorized a gentler alternative; Hell's Buddhists, fronted by a certain Asokananda (*aka* Harold Brülte, 40), a Buddhist monk and lead singer in a German band called Massenmord (Mass Murder). Hell's Buddhas are planning a five-month circumnavigation of the Indian Continent, on classic Enfield motorcycles, Nirvana-bent for leather, to 'promote peace, communal harmony, love and understanding'.

## A Day Trip into Limbo

Most Christian tour packages to Hell, from the days of the very first visionaries to Dante, have also included visits over the border to Limbo and Purgatory. **Limbo**, a real Must, has that neither-here-nor-thereish atmosphere of airport terminals, or the London Underground. As Coleridge put it:

> Wall'd round,
> and made a Spirit-jail secure,
> By the mere Horror of blank
> Naught-at-all,

On the banks of the Styx, Hell's suburb is a place where people get stuck through no fault of their own. In Roman times, it was enough not to receive a proper funeral. Over the river, next to Minos' tribunal, Virgil found a vacant lot, home to newborn babies and people put to death for crimes they did not commit.

The Christians used this lot, just inside the first circle of hell, to construct their own Limbo, and in a rare impulse of kindness they installed air-conditioning when they turned up the heat in Hell proper. There's a nursery for babies, *limbus parvulorum*, who died tainted with original sin; back in the old days they had to undergo some kind of torture for neglecting to have been baptized. Since the invention of Purgatory, the nursery hasn't had many new occupants: babies eventually work their way up to Heaven. *Limbus patrum*, an area set aside for the Patriarchs of Old Testament, is frankly a mess—vacant and vandalized after Jesus smashed down the door and kidnapped the residents; you can see the rocking chair where Abraham used to sit, holding Lazarus to his bosom, and, if you track down the Fury with the key, she'll point out the graffiti on the walls left by Isaiah, Daniel, David, Adam and Eve ('We was framed').

By far the cushiest part of the whole complex is *Limbus paganum* (the former Elysian Fields) populated by noble pagans who have been specially chosen on the idea that they probably would have been Christians if they'd had half a chance. Homer, Plato and Socrates hobnob here, 'neither joyful or doleful', clicking their worry beads and wondering what's for supper, the way old Greek men do in the *kafenion*.

Limbo, where you can chill out and celebrity spot, is the Ritz next to **Purgatory**, which tends to attract only special interest groups—spiritualists and oujii board artists, and social workers on a spree. A hot-and-bothered boot camp for the soul (seven years is the average tour of duty) there's a good deal of digging of holes and filling them in again, moving boulders about and according to *Thurkill's Vision* of 1206, an obstacle course through fire, a freezing salty lake and a bridge bristling with sharp stakes and thorns. The Mount of Joy, the BIGGEST church anywhere, big enough to contain the whole world, awaits for those who pass muster; if not, it's mandatory re-enlistment.

Purgatory staff, not bad enough for the razzle dazzle of Hell) are bureaucrats, working in conditions similar to a Jerry Lewis Telethon, taking prayers, masses and pledges from earth, some marked 'Priority Handling' by the Virgin Mary. Day in, day out the demons tally up these credits against each soul's debit of sin and relay them by loud speaker to the blasted field:

'Murphy, ten minutes out of the fire and half a warm beer!'

And so on.

# the who's who of

'D'emon' is a Greek word, *daimon*, and in the classical world it could be used for nearly any sort of spirit. Fiendish connotations only came with Christianity and Greek bibles, which used the word to translate Old Testament bogies and foreign gods frowned upon by the prophets of Israel, as well as the real demons promised in the Gospels and every sort of supernatural being from the old classical religions as well. They're all evil, said Paul and Jerome and Augustine, to Hell with them. And to Hell they dutifully went.

Lacking regular censuses, the population of Hell can only be estimated. Over the centuries a great amount of ingenuity has gone into determining the number of demons. In Roman times, old St Macarius of Alexandria had a vision where he saw demons 'as numerous as bees', but, from the Middle Ages onwards, scholars demanded more precision. They knew from whichever inspired text they chose to accept that either one half or one third of all the original angels fell with Satan, and made their calculations from there. Philosopher Michael Scot put the exact number at 14,198,580, while Alphonsus de Spina of Spain found the total to be 133, 306, 668. By the 16th century the numbers seemed to be dropping, perhaps because so many demons were busy on earth in that grisly age of Inquisitions, religious wars and witch hunts; only 66 infernal princes and 6,660,000 demons (there's that number again) were recorded.

While they were counting demons, these clever minds were also arranging them into a hierarchy that made a hellish mirror-image to the hierarchy of Heaven, or that of feudal Europe. Suddenly Hell had princes, dukes and counts, in addition to the old mumbo-jumbo of dominions, principalities and powers. Theologians and sorcerers competed to give the most comprehensive accounts of the big

# HELL

Lacking regular censuses, the population of Hell can only be estimated.

shots of Hell; many of these books survive, and they hardly ever agree on anything.

Nevertheless we can offer you an introduction to some of the leading celebrities. These, of course, are not the real names. Like all self-respecting members of the underworld, demons go by aliases. If you knew a demon's real name, you would have him in your power. ✹

## Abraxas

The demon at the top of the list is a pretty shadowy critter, one whose diabolically euphonious name gets him a mention in many fashionable incantations, though little is known of his character and misdeeds. Sometimes he has a human head, sometimes a cock's. The name is probably more important than the

demon; Abraxas is the same as abracadabra, and both go back to the Gnostics of 2000 years ago. It may be that the name of a demon got turned into a magic charm from the talismans worn to get rid of a disease or spell, by evicting the demon who caused it. The talisman would be carved:

abracadabra
abracadabr
abracadab
abracada
abracad
abraca
abrac
abra
abr
ab
a

As the name dwindled away, so would the disease. 🐾

JJ

## Adramalech

Demonologies from the Old Testament to Victorian dilettante mystics place this gent among the top ten demons; in the 16th-century Pseudomonarchia Daemonum he is the Grand Chancellor of Satan's empire. By other accounts he has become kinky in his old age: Adramalech is in charge of the Devil's wardrobe, and in his rare appearances he himself likes to take the form of a peacock. ↓

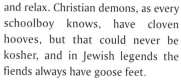

## Asmodeus

How can you tell a Jewish demon from a Christian demon? You'll have to convince it to take off its shoes

and relax. Christian demons, as every schoolboy knows, have cloven hooves, but that could never be kosher, and in Jewish legends the fiends always have goose feet.

Asmodeus, besides goose feet, has a dragon's tail, and on special holidays he appears in his full regalia of three heads, one of a ram, one of a bull, and one of a man. Originally, he was not Jewish at all, but a Zoroastrian archangel named Aeshma. At one point he was evidently weighed in the scales of the Persians and found wanting, or else the Jews simply needed another demon whose name began with A, for they bought him from the Persians for a sheep and three bags of figs. Israel was lucky to find him; thanks to the magic ring that King Solomon got from the archangel Michael, he was able to force Asmodeus to help with the building of the Temple. The demon knew knew the hiding place of the *shamir*, a worm that could split stones simply by touching them.

Later on, unfortunately, the king got a little too cosy with this useful demon. In one dark story Asmodeus tricks Solomon into giving him his throne, with terrible consequences for Israel; this story may preserve the dismay of pious fundamentalists about moral decay in Solomon's late reign, evidenced by the king's dalliances with foreign women and his permitting the building of temples to foreign gods in Jerusalem. From there, Asmodeus went on to star in the Apocryphal *Book of Tobit*, where he became so passionately enamoured of a woman named Sarah that he killed seven of her suitors before the archangel Raphael chased him off to Egypt. Since then Asmodeus has always been associated with lust, and he often takes female form to seduce men. He goes both ways, though, and he was given credit with seducing the nuns of Loudun in the famous possession scare of the 1630s, subject of a novel by Aldous Huxley, and Ken Russell's film *The Devils*.

## Astaroth

In Hell, as in most mythological Heavens, you can expect to find plenty of interesting cross-dressers. Astaroth used to be Astarte, a beautiful and powerful goddess of the Assyrians and later Phoenicians; she was the equivalent of Aphrodite or Venus. Even in her early days she hung out in the underworld (*see*

**History**, p.80), but Astarte really started to go wrong when she got involved with the Hebrews, who turned her into a very smelly demon and then insulted her; in some texts she, or rather he, was the boss of all the demons.

## Azazel

In Leviticus (16:26), God tells Aaron to find a Scapegoat, laden with the sins of the people, and lead it away and sacrifice it 'for Azazel'. This character seems to have been the head of the *se'irim*, goat-like demons that haunted waste places and worried the Israelites mightily while they were wandering in the desert. Azazel appears next in the Apocryphal *Book of Enoch*, as one of the 'Watchers', who came down to earth and taught mankind most of the evil tricks we still practice today from warfare to the men to cosmetics.

## Balam

A sort of crowned goatish demon, usually seen riding a bear. Not to be confused with the biblical Balaam (Num. 22:24) who whipped his own ass in the middle of the road.

## Beelzebub

One of the many 'baals' of the Middle East (*see* Belphegor, p.37), Baal-Zebub, the 'Lord of the Flies', is reckoned in many accounts the second-in-command down below, or else just another name for Satan himself. How he got the name is not entirely clear. One account has it that this particular Baal's idols were smeared with the blood of his sacrifices, which must have attracted a few flies.

He's a brute, this Beelzebub: big, black and hairy, with long horns and bat wings, and though he is the most sought-after infernal celebrity at black masses, all the black magic books recommend particular care if you mean to conjure him up; it's much easier to call him up than get rid of him.

## Belial

Opinions differ on this early and important member of the infernal pantheon. The name apparently means 'worthless' in Hebrew, and Belial suffered through the Middle Ages as a stock character in low sermons and mystery plays. To Milton however, he was:

*...graceful and humane;*
*A fairer person lost not Heav'n;*
*he seemd*
*For dignity compos'd and high*
*exploit.*
(*Paradise Lost*, Book II, 110-12)

He gives Lucifer prudent counsel in the conclave after the Fall, recommending that the new demons lay low for a while, and not provoke Jehovah into giving them another bashing. Belial is always whispering advice to somebody, and he usually deals with the rich and famous. According to Milton's contemporaries, he was the Devil's special minister to the Turkish sultan, helping him plan new outrages against the innocent Christians of Europe.

Often portrayed as one of the more learned demons, Belial turns up as a lawyer in many medieval stories, complaining to God that 'a certain fellow named Jesus' is robbing him of souls that rightfully belong to Hell. In most versions Jesus gets in touch with a smart Jewish lawyer—Moses himself—and wins the case, though in the 1473 *Book of Belial*, published in Augsburg, the case goes on appeal all the way up to a special judicial committee that includes Aristotle and Caesar Augustus. Jesus won this one too. He always does.

## Belphegor

'Baal', in the ancient Middle East, was not the name of an individual god, but a generic term for the agri-cultural god or reigning deity of a place. One of these, a Moabite god called Baal-Phegor, was worshipped by many Israelites for a long time, and his cult became the state religion in the time of King Ahab. Baal's priests were denounced on Mount Carmel by Elijah. King Jehu massa-cred the Baal worshippers, and Baal-Peor was demoted to the disgraceful-ly vulgar demonship he has occupied ever since. Belphegor is the demon most closely associated with shit. If the devil-worshippers in your build-ing have been smearing it all over the basement walls, it is probably Belphegor who is to blame.

## Incubi

The Devil sends these deceptively hunky male spirits, creatures of dreams, to knock up virtuous women in the dead of night when nobody's around. The result is invariably a lit-tle monster. Women in doubt should always look out for cloven hooves in an otherwise desirable specimen. The incubi have left any number of love children in our mortal plane. The Huns, all of them, were included among these, as was the wizard Merlin, and Martin Luther (that's what the Catholics said, anyway). Documented cases in modern times include Rosemary's Baby, the late President Kim Il Sung of North Korea, and many of the people with strange hair and perky smiles that we see on the television. 🔥

## Lilith

The first woman, according to the legends of the Hebrews, was also the first woman with an Attitude. According to the Haggadah, God created Adam and Lilith at the same time, meaning the two to start a nice patriarchal family. Lilith had other ideas. She thought she was as good as her man, and demanded equality and a little respect. She didn't get it. When they explained to her that the Missionary Position was the only holy way to go downtown, it was the last straw. She walked out of Adam's loving arms, out of Paradise, and into a lonely career of eternal vilification at the hands of Judaeo-Christian preachers and storytellers.

After she left, God sent angels to follow her, to try and talk her into coming home and being a good girl. She said no, so God put an everlasting curse on her and her offspring. Then he created a more submissive though devious mate for Adam (and look what happened). Lilith, meanwhile, went off to live by herself in the 'waste places'; she doesn't seem to spend much time in Hell, no doubt finding the boys down there just as backward as the ones in Paradise.

They say that Lilith dances in the ruins of lost cities, that she fools around with demons and makes more demons, that she hangs around cradles hoping to steal the babies (the word 'lullaby' is probably a charm against her). They say that she seduces poor innocent men and then kills them and throws their carcasses down to Hell. But they would say that, wouldn't they? ✋

## Mammon

A minor character, he didn't come into his own until he was discovered by the nation that would eventually make his worship into a holy philosophy: the English. In that first Hellish Parliament, in the second book of *Paradise Lost*, Mammon is one of the demons who counsels Lucifer against any more warring with Heaven; he thought there would be plenty of Gems and Gold and Magnificence in their new abode to keep them all happy. Even before Milton, though, Mammon had a major role in the second book of Spenser's *Faerie Queene*.

Sir Guyon, representing Chastity in Spenser's sprawling allegory, occupies its Second Book combatting the various aspects of Desire. After nearly succumbing to 'immodest Mirth, a Lady fresh and fayre', he finds himself in Canto VII, alone in a wilderness. Squatting among boughs and shrubs he meets 'An vncouth, saluage and vnciuile wight', with ragged clothes and coal-black hands with nails like claws. This dirty Mammon is the prototype of misers in literature ever after. Guyon disputes with him a while, but he is interested enough to follow the demon through a secret passage down to the nether regions where he kept his palace:

*Betwixt them both was but*
*a litle stride*
*That did the House of Richesse*
*from hell-mouth divide.*

Guyon spends three days roaming this infernal Scrooge McDuck money bin, with a huge monster breathing over his shoulder who would tear him to pieces if he touched or even secretly coveted a bit of it. Guyon survives, but after breathing the air of corruption for so long, when he reaches the surface again the first breath of fresh air sends him into a death-like swoon.

## Mephistopheles

One of the few demons without a Biblical pedigree, Mephistopheles only makes his appearance in the Faust legends. Luther's colleague Melancthon saw Faust's tempter as a devil in the form of a long-haired dog with red eyes, but the men of the Renaissance were ready for a new kind of demon, a debonair, sophisticated and philosophical one, and Mephistopheles evolved to fit the bill. In an age when the old medieval certainties were wearing thin, Mephistopheles came up to tickle parts of our intellectual fancy the old hairy demons could never reach. In Doctor Faustus, Christopher Marlowe defined the character and provided him with some of his most memorable lines:

> Faustus: How comes it then that thou art out of Hell?
>
> Mephistopheles: Why, this is Hell, nor am I out of it.

Shakespeare too might have tried his hand with this provocative new demon—but he couldn't. For reasons that had little to do with Marlowe, the old mystery plays were outlawed at that time, taking any other stage representation of the devil with them. Mephistopheles reappears again, of course, in Goethe's Faust, still in tune with the times. Suave and sardonic, the perfect demon for the Enlightenment, he is less concerned with seducing mortals to evil than simply letting them find the way themselves. Being the Devil after all, he knows us, and he knows our ways:

> He calls it Reason,
> and uses light celestial
>     Just to outdo the beasts
> in being bestial       ❧

## Sammael

The name suggests a more conventional sort of demon, and Sammael doesn't disappoint. He's an old weather god, etymologically close to the desert wind called the simoom, and like it he is hot, horrible and speedy. Sammael wears long, curling horns and big, leathery wings to frighten people, and he is often called upon to carry away the wicked when their hour has come. He was supposedly a consort of Lilith, and father of countless demons.       ⇓

## Succubi

These are the female counterparts of the incubi (see above). They come down in the night to trouble virtuous men and give them nocturnal emissions, and for some reason they are particularly attracted to saints. Sometimes the succubi get in a family way, and what comes out is inevitably a little monster of one form or another that just increases the demon population. That is how there got to be 133,306,688 of them.

As for the rest, we haven't room or time for them, but in Hell you are sure to meet more once-powerful Gods from the Middle East, like Abbaton, Tryphon, Ammon, and Moloch. Pensioners from the old Greek underworld still hanging on, mentioned in medieval demonologies, include Cerberus, Charon, Tantalus, and Vulcan, not to mention Apollo, who probably doesn't feel at all comfortable. Later figures like Pilate turn up as demons too, keeping company with a bizarre cast of characters straight from the medieval imagination with piquant names such as Terrytop, Charlot, Tutivillus, Lussibiaus, Lightberend, Cacodemon, and Cocornifer.

England contributed Robin Hood and Robin Goodfellow, while Germany, a nation rich in demons, gave Hell Federwisch, Frauenzorn, Hinkelbein, Heinekin, Rumpelstiltskin, Haemmerlin, Haussibut, Schonspiegel, Spiegelglanz, Hornli, Sclange, Gobli, Barbarin, Hellhundt, and Funkeldune. There's also Dusius, a Gaulish demon who undoubtedly goes back to pre-Christian times. The Gauls used to swear by him, and, occasionally, so do we—'The deuce, you say!'

Most of the above went out of fashion long ago, and it is virtually inpossible to say how they occupy their days now that people have forgotten all about them. 🐾

# touring

## What's Your Sin, Brother?

**H**ell has changed out of all recognition since Dante Alighieri began the first guide-book to it in 1306. Though no other guidebook writers will ever match its style, for our purposes the account may be as useful as a guide to pre-war Berlin, or the Soviet Union.

Dante's meticulously constructed Hell provides a fascinating mirror of the High Medieval mind. Like all educated men of his time, the poet was brought up on Aristotle and throughout his life he remained in thrall to that most insufferable of pedants. From Aristotle came the mania for endless ordering and classification: Dante's Inferno is one of the few ever invented for which a plan could be drawn (and nearly every book ever written on the *Divina Commedia* has one). Every sinner ever born is pinned exactly in his or her proper place, as if they were all specimens in the display cases of some infernal museum of natural history.

William Blake, that noted expert on infernal affairs, got a job illustrating an edition of Dante near the end of his life: '...he is not a Republican', Blake scribbled in his notebook, 'Dante was an Emperor's Man, a Caesar's Man'.

Blake didn't get it entirely right. Dante wasn't an Emperor's Man. Quite the contrary: in the politics of his time Dante was a Guelph—a Pope's Man. Hell was enemy territory to him; he never really understood it, and all too often in the Inferno he gives the impression of a little boy in Sunday school who always has his hand up with the right answer.

# Dante and Odus's Hell Gazetteer

No such accusation could ever be made against the Reverend Odus Lee Wiggins of Bateman, Oklahoma. Though at first glance he seems to be a rather conventional country preacher, Wiggins holds to some teachings that are decidedly outside the fundamentalist mainstream. He has had visions of Hell since the age of 33, when, as he tells it, ' I was underneath my car tryin' to fix a split tailpipe with a tomato can and some wire, when the jack slipped and my own car fell on me.' For years, he shared these visions only with his small storefront congregation, and through the irregular distribution of leaflets from his Divine Illusion Gospel and Tract Society. In 1995, however, the publication of his book *What's Your Sin, Brother? My Trip To Hell And Back* (Welcome Word Press, Oklahoma City) vaulted him into near-celebrity status in the southwest; since then he has made frequent appearances on radio talk shows, and as a visiting preacher in other churches and at county fairs.

Soon after his book came out, critics in Dallas and Kansas City noticed striking parallels between Wiggins's vision of Hell and the Inferno described by Dante almost 700 years ago. We noticed them too, and we were intrigued enough to visit Bateman and interview Rev. Wiggins for this book. He claims he never read the Inferno, that Dante was never on the curriculum in the Bateman public schools—but he has read it now, and he says that the similarities 'don't surprise me a bit'. Rev. Wiggins' work is a truly remarkable document, and the close parallels with Dante can have no other explanation than a serendipitous instance of divine inspiration. The Inferno has been, so to speak, updated—by a simple country preacher, giving us the most reliable guide to Hell as it exists today.

Dante begins his Inferno recalling how he lost his way in a dark forest, 'midway through life's journey'. He meets the poet Virgil, who is to be his guide through the infernal regions. As they pass through the famous gate inscribed Abandon All Hope Ye Who Enter Here, Virgil comments to Dante that here he will see 'the people whom pain stings/And who have lost the good of the intellect'. Dante's mid-life crisis, mentioned in the very first verse of the Inferno, is indeed an intellectual one; the poet has lost his ability to make sense of God's world. His Beatrice up in Heaven, who arranged the trip for him, hopes that it will help him find his way again—not by a cheap threat of hellfire, but through a lengthy reflection on those souls who became fatally trapped in the multifarious paths of Error.

learning hell

Between the gate and the River Acheron, they find themselves in an infernal antechamber, filled with a lamenting crowd of souls being constantly stung by wasps and hornets. These are the 'lukewarm' that Jesus spoke of, the people who passed their lives 'without infamy and without praise' (III, 36). Neither Heaven nor Hell will take them.

Charon the Boatman, from Greek mythology, kept on in his old job by Hell's new Christian owners, ferries Dante and Virgil over the Acheron. On the other side, they explore the first circle, Limbo, home

to the unbaptized and to the virtuous ones who had the bad luck to be born before Christianity. This is Virgil's home, and he introduces Dante to his friend Homer and other classical poets.

After his car fell on his head, Rev. Wiggins too found himself in a waste place, only with no guide from Heaven to help him on his way. When he came to the gate, a pair of shining golden arches, in place of Dante's inscription he saw a big electric sign in pastel colours reading: THANK YOU FOR NOT SMOKING. All around the entrance other signs were posted, including one that said NO BOTTLES OR CONTAINERS ALLOWED; THANK YOU FOR KEEPING HELL ALCOHOL-FREE. Another lengthy notice read: CODE OF CONDUCT FOR GUESTS; among other points, it stated that 'no soliciting of any kind will be tolerated', 'no leaflets of any kind may be distributed', and 'groups of four or more teenagers will be dispersed'.

Just inside the main gate, where Dante's antechamber of the lukewarm was located, he saw a vast asphalt-paved plain filled with queues of people in holiday attire. These were the suburbanites: Rev. Wiggins cryptically notes that 'they don't live in the town nor the country, so the Lord jus' spit them out.' The queues stretched for hundreds of miles, around snaking ropes and gates. Announcements over the public address system gave notice that faster service could now be obtained by joining the queue for gate W55 or H322 or Y907, but Odus swore that he stayed a long while and none of the queues moved an inch.

'I sorta' floated along past all that', he recalled, and finally he made his way to Charon, still faithfully running his ferry service. Odus was able to pay the fare with one shiny American penny ('best bargain in Hell', he mused; he noted that other currencies were accepted only grudgingly). Once inside, he found the first circle to be a tranquil place, with faded green walls and battered old green and white checkered linoleum, the

abode of the most dedicated followers of fashion.

Odus describes the inhabitants as 'Everybody who ever bought a new car before the old one wore out;

everybody who ever go over to their friends for coffee and peek to see what kind of coffee pot they got; everybody who ever read two lines of the fashion column without fallin' down laughin'. There they was, all wearin' blue Mao jackets, sitting on the cold ground readin' yesterday's newspapers.' We asked Odus about Limbo, which was supposed to be occupying this space, and he just laughed. 'You think Plato and Lucretius and Buddha and all the little children goin' to get stuck some bad place forever 'cause they never got baptized? Shee-it! '

*For Dante, Hell proper began with the second circle; Minos waits here, as of old, to receive sinners and send them to their appointed places. The second circle is for the lustful, and their home is beset by an unceasing tempest, a circling storm that sweeps the souls around and around in the darkness. Classical celebrities here are mostly ladies: Helen, Cleopatra and Dido, although there's room for Paris, Helen's abductor, and Tristan from the medieval legend of Tristan and Isolde.*

Rev. Wiggins told us he wasn't at all surprised to find that this circle too had found a new purpose. 'Lust is what God put us here on this planet for', he said; 'If it wasn't for a little bit of common everyday-to-day lust you wouldn't be here askin' silly questions, brother. That's what makes the world go round.' Instead, this space belongs to those who 'turn their God-given lust inside-out' and drive it towards perverted ends. Specifically, this is the circle of the poodle women, with 'hair like the ziggurats of Babylon and rusticated pink can-opener fingernails and fat mail-order solitaire rings and all the time them little dogs gripin' and droolin' and dreamin' of their next can of five-dollar nationally-advertised dog chow made of cow lips and soybean meal and monosodium glutimate.' They share the second circle with insurance agents and vacuum cleaner salesmen, whose incessant attempts at wooing are invariably rebuffed.

*Cerberus, the faithful Hound of Hell, presides over Dante's third circle, devoted to the gluttons. As gluttony is probably the least poetic of sins, Dante can find few personalities from history to place here, but he does have some fun in this Sixth Canto by finding room for several of his despised political enemies from back in Florence. The gluttons' hell is a place of eternal rain: every kind of dismal precipitation, along with some vicious hail and bitter snow, and, of course, plenty of thick, cloying mud.*

'Over in my county,' says Rev. Wiggins, 'people are stuffin' themselves every day with Pepsi Cola and Aerosol Cheese Foam and Corn Critters and Artificial Fat, but that's only 'cause they don't know any better. Gluttony here in America ain't no sin any more, it's a matter of supporting the national economy, and the suits on the teevee tell 'em they got to do it.' But Odus didn't see anybody from Bateman in the Third Circle. 'They'd be hard to pick out', he says; 'any lardbuckets that make it to Hell slim down in a hurry'.

Instead of lardbuckets, this circle seemed to belong to those whose obsessions with diet took a more modern form. Here, Odus observed equal numbers of body nazis—surfers, iron-pumpers and such—and skinny women, diet-crazed subscribers to the glossy magazines. Naked and packed together like sardines, they bob and writhe in a broad river of cold chip fat. It still rains all the time down here, which isn't helping the inmates' tans one bit.

*Dante squeezes two entire circles into Canto VII. The fourth circle belongs to the greedy, who are forced to roll great weights in opposite directions around the circle forever. Dante doesn't seem at all interested in the fifth circle, the hell of the wrathful. A boiling stream here flows down to the nearby Styx, forming a ghastly swamp where the angry and unrepentant continue their fights, punching, biting and head-butting each other in the bubbling muck.*

A demon told Rev. Wiggins that the regulations for the greedy have been changed somewhat; 'Hell, under the old rules they'd have to put nearly everybody in here, and the Boss doesn't want to let us have all that overtime.' Instead, this zone has been given over to a huge recent influx of the unforgivably contentious, divided into the Politically Correct and the Conservatives, now circling around, and tormenting each other in the same old ruts.

One responsibility the demons do have here is singling out the most belligerent partisans from each side. These get promoted down to the swamp of the wrathful in the fifth circle; there some of the truly wrathful—bikers, inner-city villains, rednecks and hooligans—are charged with giving them their initiations.

*The first five circles in Dante belonged to the 'Sins of Incontinence'—mortal, but not too serious. From this 'outer hell', though, Dante and Virgil now cross the River Styx, ferried by Phlegyas the boatman, into the City of Dis, where Hell begins to heat up.*

*The City of Dis, surrounded by a circular wall and adorned with minarets, is the 'capital' of Hell. The rebel angels who fell with Satan reside here, and they only let the worst sinners in to keep them company. When Dante and Virgil turn up they scornfully slam the door. Eventually an angel from Heaven appears and forces the demons to open the door.*

*Just inside, is the sixth circle. On a smoky plain, Dante sees a jumble of tombs and graves. Lamentations and jets of fire issue from the tombs: this is the hell of the heretics. Each one occupies a tomb with all of his followers jammed in besides, and each is 'more or less hot', depending on the extent of its occupants' theological errors. Dante meets several Florentines here; Hell is full of them. The sixth circle is separated from the seventh by the River Phlegethon. The minotaur of ancient Crete also bars the way, and Dante and Virgil have to sneak past, through a passage in the rocks.*

The City of Dis isn't what it used to be, according to Odus: 'It looked like somethin' from the distance, but while I was crossin' the river I could see already that the neighborhood's been goin' down. Most of them towers looked like they was empty. There was bricks fallin' out of the walls, windows broken and boarded up, and piles of trash just burnin' away. Reminded me of South State Street in Chicago—I got off the wrong exit from I-94 there once. Now your man Dante had a hard time gettin' in, but when I showed up the gates were wide open, and I just walked on by.'

'Now the place might not be kept up nice any more, but it sure was noisy. When I walked in there I couldn't even hear myself think.' As Odus explained, this sixth circle has become the Hell of the trash talkers. Some of the old heretics are still here, mumbling away in their boxes. Now they have been joined by a horde of hucksters, new-age prophets, talk-show hosts, policy analysts, advertising men, film critics, governmental spokespersons, fundamentalist preachers, newsreaders, authors of self-help books, makers of infomercials, UFO investigators, used-car salesmen, political pundits and at least a few travel writers.' They were all tied up together on a great big griddle, hoppin' up and down on their smokin' feet and making the worst racket I ever heard. All I could make out was snatches like "only nine ninety-five if you call today" and "the army's known about this since 1953" and "the people want closure" and "science teaches us" and "on your knees for forgiveness" and "just look at it sparkle". That gave me such a headache, I ain't been able to turn the teevee on to this day.'

**Touring hell**

In the broad seventh circle, which stinks so bad that the poets can scarcely bear to enter it, Dante's Hell starts to become a little more complicated. This circle is for those who committed deeds of violence, and it is divided into three concentric zones. The Phlegethon itself, a river of flowing blood, is the first; men who were guilty of violence against others, including celebrities such as Alexander the Great and Attila the Hun, swim in it for eternity, while centaurs patrol the banks ready to shoot them full of arrows if they attempt to climb out.

One of these gives the poets a lift across, at a ford in the bloody stream, and they discover the second zone, the Wood of the Suicides, for those whose violence was turned upon themselves. To Dante, this was a greater sin than murder, and he portrays the suicides turned into blasted, leafless trees with harpies perched on their decayed boughs—human souls symbolically reverted to a vegetable state. A yet greater sin is violence against God, or against Nature. Dante seems ill-at-ease explaining how these categories include homosexuals and usurers, but there they are, along with the blasphemers and yet more despised Florentines, in the third zone, the Ring of Burning Sand; all enjoy a constant downpour of 'fiery flakes' that fall like infernal snow.

There are still plenty of military men in the river of blood, along with 'some fellows in ski masks'. The **Wood of the Suicides** is still in use, and larger than ever; so many new arrivals have come, for the most frivolous of causes, that Rev. Wiggins reports the jaded demons have introduced woodpeckers and termites for their increased enjoyment.

The Wood of the Suicides has grown so thick that the demons have opened it to clear-cut logging, a task assigned to the developers, those gentle folk who raped the forests and fields and towns to build concrete abominations and sprawling wastelands. They are not permitted any tools, for fear they might hurt themselves. They have to squat down and use their teeth, like the noble beaver, and whenever they falter attendant wood-demons are quick to punish them with whips, pitchforks, fines and threats of lawsuits. The logs are intended for pavilions on the Ring of Burning Sand to house new recruits.

The job of constructing these pavilions belongs to the modernist architects, who are forced to hammer nails through the logs with their foreheads. Demons see to it that all their work is exactly rectilinear, down to the 1/100000th of a millimetre; this is a difficult task with logs from the Wood of the Suicides, but all transgressors are instantly punished by having to eat a wheelbarrow of wet concrete. Odus says he recognized a fellow who had designed the shopping mall near his home, and he mentioned a 'little ugly guy with big glasses' who can only have been Le Corbusier. This one has so much concrete in his system that he has become quite stiff; his colleagues have marked him off with measures and use him for a yardstick. On Hell's high holidays they get the day off, but are forced to spend the time reading each others' books, after which the demons give quizzes and lead discussion groups.

The first of the pavilions is the **House of the Bowdlerizers**, where those who have done violence to great stories are variously twisted, boiled, squeezed and skinned, while unamused, scholarly demons decide which bits of them need to be pruned or chopped off altogether. All of the censors, commissars, popularisers and expurgators are here, though Rev. Wiggins remembered that the one who howled the loudest looked like Walt Disney.

The second pavilion is the **House of the Fakers**. This is home to all the people who used their art to teach children and adults that the highest point of human achievement could be measured in gunfights, car crashes, explosions and calculated slow-motion murders. The cowboys, the cops, the thugs and the spies are all present, along with the weasling writers, producers and directors behind them. Now that the horror-flick sadists and the gangsta rappers are starting to arrive, there is little need for attendant demons. Rev. Wiggins remembers that this part of Hell was the only one that brought him to tears: 'John Wayne and James Bond were my two greatest heroes, and seeing them abused in so many hellish ways, and so frequently, well, a man could only look away...'

The third pavilion is the **House of the Bigots**, where those who robbed

others of their humanity are forced to assume the shapes of the racial caricatures they created; demons in police uniforms come around regularly to have a bit of fun with them. Two swarthy, thick-lipped inmates, hanging by their necks from tree boughs, introduced themselves to Rev. Wiggins as Ezra Pound and T. S. Eliot. 'Hasn't God ever heard of poetic licence?' they sniffed.

The fourth pavilion is the **House of the God-Pesterers**. 'Anybody who ever prayed for a Mercedes-Benz, anybody who ever asked God to vanquish their enemies, and especially everybody who spent their lives worryin' about the salvation of their precious little souls instead of doin' the right thing 'cause it was the right thing,' Rev. Wiggins explained, 'gets to come down here and learn nine-thousand-and-ninety-nine reasons why they were mistaken.'

There were too many other pavilions for Odus to visit them all. He did, however, remember a curious one that was still under construction at the time, with glass walls, and a number of rather shockingly intimate tortures being installed inside. A signboard out in front proclaimed that this is to be the **Motel of the Special Prosecutors**.

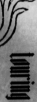
touring hell

The Ring of Burning Sand is too hot for Dante and Virgil to cross, but the presiding monster of the eighth circle or 'malebolge', obligingly comes to carry them across. This is Geryon, 'he who corrupts the whole world', a personification of Fraud. Deception, to Dante, is much worse than violence. He is obsessed with it, in fact, and nearly half of the Inferno (Cantos XVIII–XXX) is devoted to detailing the malebolgia. The word means 'evil chasms', and there are ten of them, in concentric rings, with stone bridges like spokes passing over them towards the climax of the Inferno, the great Pit at the centre. Briefly, the tour includes:

↓ seducers and panderers, marching naked while demons whip them on.

↓ flatterers, floundering about in a malebolgia full of excrement.

↓ simonists: corrupt princes of the Church, planted head first in holes with fire burning the soles of their feet.

↓ sorcerers and fortune-tellers, with their heads twisted around backwards, and tears running down their bottoms.

↓ crooked public officials, floating in a river of boiling pitch that reminds Dante of the Arsenal in Venice.

↓ hypocrites, most of them monks, condemned to wander in thick leaden cloaks.

↓ thieves, tortured by an impressive variety of serpents; when the mood strikes them they blast a sinners to ashes,

though these just as quickly reassume their shapes.

↓ deceivers, each enveloped in a living flame. Notable among these is Odysseus.

↓ schismatics, sowers of religious discord, all hacked nearly into bits, but still conscious and suffering as much as they can. Dante could hardly leave out Mohammed, and he tells the poet he's sorry he was such a Muslim.

↓ falsifiers, a mixed bag of alchemists, perjurers, counterfeiters, all afflicted with colourful wasting diseases.

From Rev. Wiggins's report, it seems clear that Hell has been continuing the old Dantean policy of using this spacious corner to dump all the categories of sinners that don't fit in anywhere else. These include:

◊ electric guitar players. 'Didn't see any good blues men down there,' Odus said, 'just the ones that play that kid crap you hear on the radio. The demons have figured out you can get better sounds puttin' electricity through musicians than you can puttin' it through instruments. And by the way,' he added, 'tell your readers they can stop lookin' for Elvis'.

◊ the Swiss. Odus, who has never been to Switzerland, doesn't understand this one, but he swears that every last one of them ends up here, in a very messy and germ-ridden *malebolgia*, stuck head-first in individual pits full of melted cheese.

⚅ folks that kept bad dogs, especially pit bulls and dobermans. This is a clean, well-lighted circle with lots of room to run. Inmates can bring their pets with them to the underworld, only upon arrival the owners are transformed into rabbits.

⚅ parking wardens and meter maids, suspended by their hands from towing hooks. On Hell's high holidays anyone else in Hell can come down here and give them forty free whacks.

⚅ structuralists, and various other Modern Critics. None of the demons could figure out who these dweebs were, and they didn't do a very good job of explaining themselves either. The demons got tired of listening to them, so finally they just filled up this *malebolgia* with cement.

⚅ cut-rate dictators. Spanish is the *lingua franca* here, though demonic tour guides pointed out to Odus a cosmopolitan cast including Generalissimo Franco, Huey Long, Marshal Pilsudski, Mussolini, Porfirio Diaz, Admiral Tojo, General Trujillo, Oliver Cromwell, Park Chung Hee, Syngman Rhee, Napoleon III, Marshal Mobutu and Mayor Daley (senior) of Chicago. Though naked, they wear all their medals pinned to their chests (because merit is recognized even in Hell), while they spend their days in the freezing cold, sitting at separate tables playing solitaire.

⚅ abstract impressionists, armed with mops and scrub brushes; demons sit on the walls flicking paint (and other substances) down below, and the perpetrators of this century's greatest intellectual fraud have got to clean them up *pronto*, or they're going to catch Hell for it.

⚅ Ford Men. This *malebolgia*, home to factory owners, engineers, efficiency experts, bean counters, economists, industrial theorists and inventors of useless gadgets, consists of a single gigantic assembly line running clear around the circle. A demon foreman explained to Odus that whatever one man screws on, somebody on the opposite end of the circle has to screw back off. The line never stops; speedups are company policy, and there is no union.

⚅ plumbers. Nobody who has ever had to call one would be surprised to find plumbers. The drains in this fetid zone are extremely backed up, and there is no beer.

⚅ lawyers. Rev. Wiggins shook his head, and said that 'what goes on in there is too gruesome to tell'.

After all this, Dante and Virgil are ready to scrape the very bottom. The ninth circle, at first glance, appears to be a walled city surrounded by towers; his companion explains that these are fifty giants frozen in place—the Titans who rebelled against Zeus back in the dream-time of mythology. One of these, Antaeus, lifts the poets down into the ninth circle.

Surprisingly, the lowest depths of hell are distinctly chilly; they are reserved for those guilty of the cold crimes of traitors—betrayed their city or country, is named for Antenor the Troja. Those who break the sacred laws of hospitality are confined in the Ptolomea, while the lowest of the low, the very bottom of Hell, is the Giudecca, named for Judas, and reserved for those who betrayed their lords. Spiritual or secular, it doesn't matter to Dante. Judas himself shares the place of honour with Brutus and Cassius.

The Inferno ends with a definite anticlimax. We meet Satan, but instead of the

in the intrigue-filled world of the 14th-century Italian city-states, spectacular treachery was all too common.

The ninth circle is the icebound River Cocytus, into which all the other infernal rivers flow. The circle is divided into four parts, all filled with more of Dante's contemporaries. The first is called Caina, for Cain, and holds those whose treason was directed against their own families. The second, Antenora, for those who lively devils of modern times, or of the medieval mystery plays, we see a numb, impotent giant form, his lower half frozen in the ice of Cocytus. Without much further comment, Dante and Virgil climb up his body, using his long hair for a grip; from there they find a passage in the rocks back to daylight—they have passed straight through the earth, and surfaced at the mountain of Purgatory in the Antipodes.

Not much in the ninth circle has changed since Dante's time. Odus remarks that one seemingly new inhabitant of Antenora, wearing an L. A. Dodgers' baseball cap and nothing else, recognized him as a fellow American and called out to him from the ice: 'Tell the people you saw Walter O'Malley in Hell. Tell 'em I shoulda' stood in Brooklyn.'

When Odus makes it to the very centre, to the pit, he is in for quite a surprise. It would be best to let him finish the story in his own words, just as he told it to us:

'Well, I walked all over that ice, slippin' and slidin', and finally I come right up to that big Devil himself, all three heads of him. Now, after all I seen I wasn't a bit afraid any more, so I just smiles and says, "Well you ol' Devil, here we are just you and me." And did I jump when the Devil answered. There was a roar like thunder——man! And he says "IF I WAS YOU I'D BE WONDERING HOW I WAS GOING TO GET THE HELL OUT OF HERE." All of a sudden the smoke started rollin' up and the blue lights were flashin' and the ground was quakin' and the demons was screamin'. Well, I got scared then, and I went and hid behind a chunk o' ice.

'Then I happened to look over on the side, and I saw this little booth hidden away, with a curtain over the doorway and all these wires and cables coming out of the top. So I got a little suspicious, and I sneaked over there while all the time that big Devil was yellin' out threats and curses at me. I pulled back the curtain and there was this little fellow in a cape and a pointy hat with moons and stars all over it, and a white beard that went most down to his knees. He was pullin' levers and throwin' switches, and it was pretty clear he'd been runnin' that big Devil that was yellin' at me. So I grabs him by the sleeve and hollers "Who the hell are you ?" And he stands there lookin' at me like a skunk caught in the headlights and he hollers back, "Zoroaster's my name. Who the hell are you ?"

'Well, I been some places and seen some things, but never anything like goin' down to the bottom of Hell and havin' a chat with the ol' Prophet Zoroaster himself. He said he was sorry for tryin' to bamboozle me with all them special effects, but he had a job to do just like anybody else. Seems he got sent down here for scarin' the daylights out of the Persians with all that good-and-evil talk. In fact, they originally built the place just for him, but it was a good thing they built it so big—he made so many followers through the ages, and most all of them have to come down here with him. Zoroaster told me he made up all that dualistic philosophy 'cause his dad used to smack him around, and wouldn't let him play ball with the other kids. He's sorry he did it too; he said if he had his life to live over again, instead of a Prophet next time he'd rather be a sailor.

'I asked him where was Hitler and all the other top-flight villains I expected to see down here. He said neither Hitler nor Napoleon nor Stalin ever set foot in Hell; they ain't nowhere. Sometimes even the Creator realizes he made a mistake. "Besides", he says, "can't you see that all this ain't nothing but a humbug hallucination and it's your own damn fault for having it?" "Point taken," I says. Then

I asked him if there was really a Devil and he said sure there was, but he ain't been down here since about Grant's second term. He told me that the Devil just got tired of this place, plain and simple, and now mostly he splits his time between New York and St-Tropez.

'Then me and Zoroaster sat down inside and had a cup of coffee and some of those sweet cakes—like they used to make back home in Persia, he said. We talked about a lot of things, about Heaven and Purgatory and Mars and Pluto and places like that; I'm not going to tell you everything he told me, but you wouldn't believe some of the things folks think are true that really are. I'm writin' them all up in my next book, which should be hittin' the supermarkets some time next July. After a while I thanked him for the joe and the information, and told him to keep up the good work, and I said it was about time I was gettin' back home. He said all right, fine with me, and took out his magic wand and waved it around and next thing I knew I was back sittin' on my own front porch. Just like that!'

# parallel

Some peoples of the earth have managed to get by just fine without any Hell at all: most of the Africans, and the North American Indians, though even they often find it necessary to slip a little Purgatory into their cosmos to discourage backsliding. Still, for us westerners a universe without a nice blazing Hell and a competent Devil wouldn't

**with all the choices it might prove difficult to find the Hell that's right for you**

seem quite right; we would worry that somehow the Big Issues were not being addressed.

Planning one's retirement can be a weighty affair. And it can be complex. The world's religious experience has created a dazzling array of possible Hells, and with all the choices it might prove difficult to find the Hell that's right for you. Here is a select

list, including the most popular foreign models, along with a few of our particular favourites.

## Chinese Hell

Since the earliest times, the Chinese seem to have had an idea of the afterlife close to that of many Western cultures. Over two thousand years ago, they buried their dead along with everything they would need to be comfortable in the tomb. Instead of seeing death as simply the point where a body and a soul parted company, though, they believed in a different sort of dispersal of the being's vital forces. In China you had two souls, a *hun* and a *po*, masculine and feminine, *yang* and *yin*. The masculine *hun* soul went out into the universe, and with the proper rites it could be convinced to inhabit a stone in a family shrine, for descendants to honour and consult. The feminine *po* went down to an underworld called the Yellow Springs—if all went well, that is. If its owner had met a violent

# HELLS

## where to stay : a select range of the alternative hells

### —a lot like China

or unjust end, if the coffin were badly oriented, the *po* could linger as a ghost, which for the Chinese would be considerably worse than any imaginable underworld.

From the 2nd century BC onwards, the Yellow Springs evolved into one of the most sprawling and complex Hells ever imagined. Partly this was a result of Buddhist influence, though it also mirrored the tendency in Chinese life to identify the Imperial government with an all-encompassing natural system that applied to the Heavens themselves as much as it did to China. Distinctions were blurred between the Emperor who reigned on earth, and the Celestial Emperor Shang Di, or Yu Huang, ruler of the entire universe. Just as earthly emperors stood at the top of a hierarchy of bureaucrats, the Supreme Ruler maintained balance and harmony in the cosmos through his own governmental machine manned by spirits and powers down to the kitchen gods of each individual home.

To this, the Buddhists contributed two important ideas. First, the principle of reincarnation and the rebirth of the soul. Hell was never a place of permanent imprisonment, but only a punishment designed to fit the magnitude of one's sins. Secondly, a tremendously elaborate system of Hells and sub-Hells had to be devised so that each sinner would have a place perfectly fitted for him.

Perhaps unique on this planet, this is a Hell invented not for lawyers, but by them. Every 'i' is dotted, and every 't' crossed, as the bewildered soul is dragged into a shadowy underworld nightmare of ordinances and regulations, mandates and petitions, sentences and demonic bailiffs. Judicial cases cross the boundaries of the living and dead worlds with unsettling ease. In ancient Chinese stories, a woman is unjustly executed and becomes a ghost, but in that state she is able to bring a case against the judge responsible and have him executed in turn; a man who commits suicide is brought back to life by the successful petition of a colleague who resents him getting out before his time and leaving him behind to do all the work.

Of course, the real beneficiaries of this legalistic labyrinth were not lawyers, but the Buddhist clergy, the only fellows who understood the system. If you were worried about what prayers to say, or which rites to perform for yourself or your loved ones, you had to consult the professionals—and we can imagine their services didn't come cheap.

Hell in Chinese is *di yu*, the 'Prisons of the Earth', and it is a place so large and varied it deserves a guidebook in itself (the Chinese have contributed plenty over the centuries, notably the 11th-century *Yuli Chaozhuan*). It is divided into ten courts, and each of these into sixteen wards. A king rules each infernal court, and the most important of these is Yanluo Wang, King of the Fifth Court. Another member of the hierarchy, the Thunder God Lei Kung, has the special charge from Heaven of dealing with particularly serious crimes on earth. Appearing with a bird's head and claws, and carrying a hammer and a drum, he comes down to destroy the evil ones, or if the workings of the spirit bureaucracy grind too slowly and he arrives late, he will be content to blast their tombs with thunder.

With its inscrutable officialdom and its parodies of jails and courts on earth, Chinese Hell is a place where Franz Kafka would feel entirely at home. Everybody seems to go there, and the reasons why are never really made clear. But at the moment of death Hell's officers come for you, bearing warrants, and lead you down through one of the many entrances to the underworld known in China. Some of these have fixed locations, mostly caves, though a temporary gate to Hell can also be concealed inside a dust storm. In the Qin and Han dynasties, under Buddhist influence, sacred Mount Tai on the Shandong peninsula became a sort of administrative centre for departed souls, where the courts would decide each fate.

Unlike Christians, the Chinese never get too excited about their future in Hell. After all, it isn't permanent, and for them the Heavenly alternative is not nearly as desirable as in western religions. If Hell is China, Heaven is China too, and it is usually portrayed as a spirit-world counterpart of the Imperial court, with a rigid hierarchy, a tiresome court etiquette and plenty of kow-

> **In any Chinese grocery you can purchase stacks of 'spirit money'. usually inscribed BANK OF HELL**

towing and scraping to the celestial big shots.

As screwy as the Chinese afterlife might seem to a western mind, there is something in their peculiarly logical and down-to-earth dispensation that can be very attractive. As they always do, the Chinese are saying that life is everything. If we have to suffer a patently absurd spell in the shadow world, so be it; the impor-

tant thing is that when it's over we'll be back ready to live and love and do the whole silly business over again. For religion, the only remaining concern is that part of the soul that stays behind in the spirit world. If you can't escape China even by dying, neither can you escape your family; your fate and theirs are still inextricably intertwined. The dead can exert a positive influence in the affairs of their descendants, who in turn have a responsibility to sustain the departed souls by means of sacrifices.

The Chinese may no longer kit out their dead in the Egyptian manner, but they have found some more economical means of taking care of them: for example, burning specially-made paper clothes so the departed will have something new to wear. But as on earth, the most practical and useful gift is money, and the Chinese have found a way to arrange this too. In any Chinese grocery you can purchase stacks of 'spirit money'. usually inscribed BANK OF HELL, in Chinese and English, and they bear the portrait of Yanluo Wang, the most virtuous of the ten kings that judge the dead. They might also stock Bank of Hell coins and gold ingots, and to keep up with the times there are now infernal credit cards and travellers' cheques. Hell money has other purposes besides keeping your grandfather in cigarettes down below—you can also use it to buy off bothersome ghosts.

Being above all a reflection of what is happening on earth, Chinese Hell is always changing to keep up to date. Reports come in from time to time, by means of spirit writing, concerning the state of affairs down below. One of the most popular of these is a book called *Journey to Hell*, which appeared in Taiwan in 1978 and has already sold over five million copies. The *Journey to Hell* notes that 'since worldly people have adopted modern behaviour patterns, the netherworld has added many new halls of punishment'. One of these was created especially for foreign missionaries; above its gate is an inscription, 'All Teachings Return to Unity'. Here the inhabitants, mainly Bible-thumping Christians one suspects, get to sample Hell Chinese-style in return for having disparaged and mocked it during their lives. That'll learn 'em.

## Buddhism: Hot Hells and Cold Hells

Nothing could be more noble, more true, than the spiritual insights and teachings of Gautama Buddha. This gentleman found out the hard way, some 2,500 years ago, that life is suffering. He saw this suffering as the result of our worldly illusions, and in his fashion he attempted to tell us what to do about it. Buddha did not care much for philosophical speculations, or guesses of what the afterlife might have in store for us. The whole point of Buddhism was to find a way to jump off the endless, dreary cycle of karma and reincarnation, but

wherever Buddhism flourished its clergy found that nirvana was a little too difficult and ambitious for the average Joe. Joe knew his limitations, and he was usually resigned to another bittersweet and imperfect life, and another one after that. He wanted to know more about the space in between, the afterlife, and the Buddhist monks gave him more than he bargained for.

When you go down to meet Yama, the fearsome Tibetan judge of the dead, you will also meet the monkey-headed Shinje, holding the scales in which your fate is decided. Black pebbles on one side for the bad deeds, and white pebbles on the other for the good ones. There are six different places they can send you to be reincarnated, six 'pathways': the realm of *devas*, for the spiritually advanced, and then in descending order that of human beings, of animals, of evil spirits, of 'hungry ghosts, and finally, for the truly vile, of Hell. The Tibetan tradition is one of the simpler ones; there are only eight Cold Hells (for impious acts done by calculation) and eight Hot Hells (for the same acts committed in anger). In other lands they count as many as 128 hot Hells, 8 cold Hells, and 84,000 in between.

Tibetan painters have left some fascinating scenes of the various Hells and their torments, which can be as cruel or silly as anything the West has dreamed up. In one Hell we see prostitutes getting molten metal poured down their throats, while in another, monastic students who skimmed carelessly through their texts get squashed under a gigantic holy book.

In every land where Buddhism flourished, in fact, scenes of Hell became a popular subject for painters. The Nara National Museum, in that city that was a medieval capital of Japan, has some fine examples painted on a scroll called the *Jigoku Zoshi*. One shows the condemned floating in an ocean of excrement, tormented by whiskered maggots. Another, depicting a Hell for crooked merchants, shows them spending their days sorting flaming coals into boxes; in a third, demons grind thieves to powder in the Hell of the Mortars. Sellers of unclean food get a Hell of Pus and Blood full of huge nasty bugs, while arsonists enjoy the erupting gases of the Hell of Smoke. Best of all, for cruelty to animals, there is the Hell of the Cock, where a giant, fire-breathing chicken squeezes malefactors in its claws— lab experimenters, one would hope,

> Best of all, for cruelty to animals, there is
> the Hell of the Cock, where a giant, fire-breathing
> chicken squeezes malefactors in its claws

and ladies who pestered their husbands for fur coats—and gets them ready for a barbeque.

Buddhist Hell is the perfect Hell for the cynical. After all, Judge Yama, and Shinje, and the hot Hells and cold Hells and all their torments, are part of the great illusion too, just like everything in our living world. If we could only be strong and remember that, as the Tibetan *Book of the Dead* advises, then the illusion would shatter and we would be free.

## The Islamic Pit

On one thing Christians and Muslims can agree; sinners are going to burn. As befits the simplest of the world's great religions, Islam presents our choices for the afterlife in an utterly straightforward manner, and in terms that no Southern Baptist would find anything to disagree with except the identity and religion of the damned.

References to Hell, or to the Old Testament *Gehenna*, are sprinkled liberally through the Koran, and the place is never anything else but searingly hot.

Infidels get quick service. As soon as you are buried, you will be visited by two angels named Munkar and Nakir. They will force you to sit up in the grave and question you as to your faith, and if you don't tell them that God is One, and that Muhammad is his Prophet, you get the '*adhab al-qabr*', the 'torment of the tomb'. As for what happens to true believers, there are differences of opinion in the various traditions of Islam. Some hold that the good and the wicked get their just desserts immediately, while others speak of a dreamlike state of limbo called *barzakh*, which lasts until the Day of Judgement. Interestingly, on that day it is the Prophet Jesus who descends to preside over the end of the world, just as he does in the *Book of Revelations*. In a reminiscence of earlier faiths, the souls are then weighed in the balance, and 'he whose deeds weigh light in the Balance shall plunge in the womb of the pit'.

Islam, on the whole, manages to avoid the sort of morbid preoccupation Christians have always had with detailing the tortures of Hell. As the Koran repeats over and over Hell is a blazing fire, and that is usually all. It does have one advantage over the Christian Hell; at least you get refreshments. The damned eat the fruit of a tree called *er-Zakkoum*, which grows in the root of Hell and blossoms with demons' heads; perhaps this is the true face of the forbidden tree in Paradise. And to wash it down there will be a choice of boiling water, molten copper and pus. All you can drink.

Islam has its counterpart to the Devil in Iblis, the name of an old Arabian demon whose name means 'despair'. He is also known as Shaytan—the same word as Satan—and there's no doubt that this is essentially the same Old Accuser. Like Satan, he was thrown out of Heaven early on, though not for outright rebellion against God. When God made Adam, he ordered the angels to bow down before his new creation, and Iblis, full of pride, refused. So he has good reason to be man's eternal enemy. The Sufis, however, say Iblis refused to pay homage to Adam because he loved Allah too much to bow to another being— Allah, after all, had ordered his angels not to worship anyone else.

Iblis it was who tempted Eve in the garden, though in the Muslim version he asks all the animals to smuggle him into Paradise, and only the accursed serpent agreed. Iblis sneaked in, concealed in the snake's mouth, which proved a perfect pulpit from which to do his evil whispering. Like all the angels, Iblis is both male and female, but he has the unique ability to impregnate himself (don't ask how), and that is how he created all the lesser demons that tempt us and plague us. ❀

**It does have one advantage over the Christian Hell; at least you get refreshments.**

Our English name for the Last Resort comes from the Old Teutonic *Hel*, 'to cover or conceal', and its most memorable description was put down over half a century before Dante by the great Icelander Snorri Sturluson (*c*. 1179–1241) in the *Prose Edda*. According to Snorri, Earth itself is descended from Hell (*Niflheim*), the underworld of the dead located in the far north.

Niflheim had a great well, the source of eleven rivers, which froze and filled Ginnungagup, the cosmic void. South of Niflheim, however, there was an extremely hot world called Muspell. Sparks from Muspell fell on the rivers, and the melted drops coalesced to create the giant Ymir and the primordial cow, Audumbla, who supplied Ymir with milk. As Ymir sweated, his perspiration formed other giants, both male and female.

Meanwhile, the cow Audumbla licked blocks of ice and shaped them into the first man, Buri. Buri's son, Bor, marries Bestla, daughter of a giant, Bolthorr, and together they produce the gods Odin, Vili, and Ve. These three kill Ymir and fashion the Earth out of his body with all his fertile BO as part of the package. In the centre sprouts the great tree of life, Yggdrasil, supported by three roots. One root reaches north to Niflheim, another root goes east to Jotunheim, the world of the frost-giants, and another south to blazing Muspell. In the centre of these is Middle Earth, the world of humans.

Niflheim was the lowest of nine worlds, all of which were ruled by Hel, the goddess of death. Hel's mother was the trickster giant Loki; turning into a woman at will was only one of the tricks up his sleeve. Hel had a hideous body—half black and

## Hel was bleak, shadowy, cold, dark, foggy and boring, rather like Oslo in November

rotting, and half blue with cold. Delay and Slowness were Hel's attendants, while she ate at a table called Hunger, cut her meat with the knife Starvation, and lay down on a bed named Care.

As in Greek Hades, the entire Norse underworld eventually took her name, and, although not *per se* a place of punishment, Hel was bleak, shadowy, cold, dark, foggy and boring, rather like Oslo in November

There are a few dragons, associated with buried treasure, one of whom, 'Corpse eater' Nidhogg, lives on a boiled potage of Viking enemies. Hel is visited by Balder, the son of Odin and the goddess Frigg. Balder was beloved of the men and gods for his goodness and justice, and held court, where he settled the legal disputes of gods and men. But Balder dreams he will die and tells his mother, Frigg, and Frigg demands the solemn oath of fire and water, bird and beast, earth, stones, and metals that they will not harm her darling son. The gods then began to play with Balder,

throwing darts and stones at him, knowing that because of the oath Balder would remain unharmed.

Then mischievous Loki happens by, and, disguising himself as a woman, asks Frigg why Balder suffers no harm. Frigg tells him, and lets him on her secret: she failed to obtain the oath from the mistletoe. Loki at once brings in some mistletoe and offers it to the Hoder, the blind brother of Balder, offering to guide his aim so that he, too, can play the game. Balder, pierced by the mistletoe, falls dead, and ends up in the land of Hel.

In dismay, Odin sends his messenger, Hermod, to the underworld to ask Hel to release Balder. Hermod must cross the river on the Echoing Bridge guarded by Modgud, the skeleton woman, then ride through the Iron Wood where the trees have sharp metal leaves. Sleipnir, the eight-legged steed, takes Hermod over the gate into the walled city of Hel, avoiding Garm, the dog of the bleeding breast who guards the gate. Hel, however, will only free Balder if everything in the world, dead or alive, will weep for him. The gods send messengers throughout the world requiring all nature, to weep for Balder. All do, except a giantess named Thokk (Loki in disguise),

Odin with Sleipnir, the eight-legged horse

forcing Balder to stay in Hel.

The furious gods chain Loki as punishment, although it is foretold that one day the mischief-maker will break the chains. This will be the sign for the loosing of all evil, monsters and giants, who will attack the gods in the great battle of Ragnarok, the twilight of the gods. Earth will be destroyed by fire, and the entire universe will sink back into the sea. This final destruction will be followed by a rebirth, the Earth re-emerging from the sea, fresh and green.

The Vikings deserve a special mention for making their Heaven, Odin's hall, Valhalla, an even less attractive proposition than their Hel. The only way to get there is to be slain in battle, from where a Valkyrie will whisk you off in her flying chariot to Valhalla, where every night you can expect a hoedown with Odin (the menu, however, is limited: meat from Schrimnir the boar and mead from the udder of Heldrun the goat). Then it's up every morning to don battle gear and merrily hack each other to pieces. But every evening you'll be put back together again, to consume more boar chops and fermented honey, until the end of time.

## Milton's Inferno: Hell as High Art

By a truly diabolical irony, it took a Puritan poet to create the most lavish, most gorgeously detailed Hell of all time. Reciting Paradise Lost aloud to his secretary from the prison of his blindness, Milton conjured up an entirely new Hell, a world of 'darkness visible' as far removed from the one-dimensional pizza-oven Hells of medieval legend as it was from Heaven itself. Three centuries of uncomfortable schoolchildren have felt the heat and smelled the sulphur.

After the fall from Heaven, at the end of the first book, Lucifer and his crew pick themselves up, dust themselves off, and get ready to start all over again. But first, to demonstrate their own fatal vanity, and to give the poet a chance to work in some brilliant descriptive verse, they build themselves a palace. Following classical convention, Hell had to have one, and Milton's is far bigger and grander than anything old Greek Hades ever possessed, a worthy rival to the palace Louis XIV was building at the same time in Versailles.

This palace, the 'home of all devils', added a new word to the language— Pandaemonium. Its first function was to host the devils' first Parliament.

The muscular Miltonian Protestant God was no patsy, and Satan's host needed to plan whether to keep up the fight, or simply lay low and hope to survive. The entirely modern nature of Milton's Lucifer becomes clear right from the beginning, with his remarkable opening address:

*Powers and Dominions,*
*Deities of Heav'n,*
*For since no deep*
*within her gulf can hold*
*Immortal vigor,*
*though oprest and fall'n,*
*I give not Heav'n for lost.*

This devil is about defiance. 'My sentence is for open Warre,' he says, and with his darkly magnificent refusal to bow to the necessities of Goodness and Light he turns a new page in the psychology of the western mind. William Blake, perhaps the first to understand what was really at stake, got it right when he wrote that, 'The reason Milton wrote in fetters when he wrote of Angels & God, and at liberty when of Devils & Hell, is because he was a true Poet, and of the Devil's party without knowing it.'

## Bad Bill Blake's Hell for Heroes

Blake himself, next in the line of great English poets after Milton, had no doubt as to which party owned his allegiance. Like the Romantic poets of his time, he wrote from outside the Christian tradition, but while contemporaries such as Shelley and Byron lost themselves in foreign travel and classical mythology, Blake stayed home in London, and never strayed far from the old Biblical themes, spinning out of them an original mythology of his own.

Blake lived in a wild, iconoclastic era, the time of the Romantics and the American and French Revolutions, and though little-noticed while he lived, he was preparing a major revolution of his own, proclaiming a liberation of the spirit more serious and thorough than anything Voltaire, Rousseau or Jefferson ever dreamed. Rejecting all the superstition and dismal doctrines of organized religion, he nevertheless studied the visions of past prophets to see what was really behind them.

> 'Energy (called 'evil') rises from the subconscious ('Hell'), restricted by reason ('good'), product of the superego ('Heaven').'
>
> *Blake's Dictionary*,
> S. Foster Damon

To Blake, there are angelic and infernal ways of looking at everything. Truth does not lie with one or the other, but with the dynamic tension between the two. And as his concern was with liberating mankind from what he described as the 'mind-forged manacles' of repressive, analytical ways of thinking, he usually chose to come at his subjects from the devil's point of view.

*We both read the Bible day & night*
*But you read black*
*where I read white.*

There is no better introduction to the Blakean upside-down world than the hallucinatory *Marriage of Heaven and Hell* (1790–93), a series of etchings accompanying some of the poet's own trips to Hell and some stranger places, recounted in a mixture of prose and verse. There's a little bit of everything: principles of infernal philosophy, conversations with Isaiah and Ezekiel, Proverbs of Hell, a visit to a printing house down below, and best of all a dispute between Blake and an Angel, who appears offering some conventionally pious warnings about the future of the poet's soul. Blake asks to be shown what his eternal lot will be, and the Angel takes him through a stable and into a church, down the church vault, which led into a mill, which led into a cave; they followed this until they reached an immense grotto, where they hung from the roots of trees and observed the dark expanse below:

W. Blake  *Satan calling up his legions*

By degrees we beheld the infinite Abyss, fiery as the smoke of a burning city; beneath us, at an immense distance, was the sun black but shining; round it were fiery tracks on which revolv'd vast spiders, crawling after their prey, which flew, or rather swum, in the infinite deep, in the most terrific shapes of animals sprung from corruption; & the air was full of them, & seem'd composed of them: these are Devils, and are called Powers of the air. I now asked my companion which was my eternal lot? he said: 'between the black & white spiders.'

In the midst of the infernal vision, in 'a cataract of blood mixed with fire', the tremendous biblical monster Leviathan appears, his forehead 'divided into streaks of green and purple like those on a tyger's forehead.' The Angel is frightened and flees, but as soon as he is gone, Blake finds himself,

...sitting on a pleasant bank beside a river by moonlight, hearing a harper, who sung to his harp; & his theme was: "The man who never alters his opinion is like standing water, and breeds reptiles of the mind."

Accustomed, after so many centuries, to obedience and respect from good Christians, the Angel is hardly prepared for what happens next. Blake finds him again, picks him up and carries him off to show the Angel his own fate. He takes him out beyond the bounds of the solar system, into the silent, dead void of space:

'Here,' said I, 'is your lot, in this space—if space it may be called.' Soon we saw the stable and the church, & I took him to the altar and open'd the Bible, and lo! it was a deep pit, into which I descended, driving the Angel before me; soon we saw seven houses of brick; one we enter'd; in it were a number of monkeys, baboons & all of that species, chain'd by the middle, grinning and snatching at one another, but withheld by the shortness of their chains: however, I saw that they sometimes grew numerous, and then the weak were caught by the strong, and with a grinning aspect, first coupled with, & then devour'd, by plucking off first one limb and then another, till the body was left a helpless trunk; this, after grinning & kissing it with seeming fondness, they devour'd too; and here and there I saw one savourily picking the flesh off of his own tail...'

Few of Blake's writings offer such tidy examples of his talent for what one critic has called the 'rhetoric of shock', but the poet drops a clue as to what he really intends. After this strange exchange of visions, Blake and the Angel accuse each other of imposing; Blake opines that 'it is only lost time arguing with you whose works are only Analytics'. As always in his work, ideas are living things; the simian lovelies probably represent the hypocritical dogmas of the Angel's faith, the deathly organized religion that is the soul's real Enemy.

Blake's conclusion to the vision is straightforward enough: 'Opposition is True Friendship.' His poetical energy delights above all in argument, and being the poet after all he gets to write the end to this one:

*Note: This Angel, who is now become a Devil, is my particular friend; we often read the Bible together in its infernal or diabolical sense, which the world shall have if they behave well.*
*I have also the Bible of Hell, which the world shall have whether they will or no.*

## West Hell

The United States, still a relative baby among the world's nations, has nevertheless managed to build up a substantial body of folklore. And nowhere is it more suspicious than in the tales and behaviour attributed to African Americans. Southern Blacks in the old days certainly had no doubt as to who the devil was, and when he came around in the guise of some earnest young fellow looking for authentic folk tales, they were likely to tell him just about anything. Thus began the peculiar legend of the 'Negro paradise', the mythical Doo Wah Diddy, or Diddy Wah Diddy. This place became nationally famous from continual mentions on Jack Benny's radio show in the 40s.

There's a huge joke lurking here, and the key to it can be found in examining old song lyrics, especially blues songs, which contain some of the choicest sexual double-entendres ever conceived on this planet. A later version might help to elucidate the matter:

*There's a place down south called Doo Wah Diddy*
*It ain't no town and it ain't no city*
*But me oh my, it sure is pretty*
*Doo Wah Diddy*

The country blacks of Dixie were equally willing to jive a sophisticated black author like Zora Neale Hurston, who roamed through her native Florida in the Depression collecting tales for the Federal Writers' Project of the WPA. They told her about West Hell, a neighbourhood which was some miles west of Regular Hell. This was the worst part of Hell, and only the worst villains were sent to it. Even the Devil didn't like to send any of his demons there for fear they might get hurt.

Now **John-de-Conqueror** came through Hell one day (he's a heroic figure from many stories, and also a personification of High John the Conqueror, or St Johnswort, an herb considered a sovereign charm against evil). John fell in love with the baby girl child from among the Devil's many daughters, and she agreed to elope with him. They stole the Devil's prize horses, named Hallowed-be-Thy-Name and Thy-Kingdom-Come, and started off, but the Devil heard about it...

*He overtook the lovers in West Hell and they fought all over the place, so good a man, so good a devil! But way after while John tore off one of the Devil's arms and beat him, and married the Devil's daughter... If you don't believe he done it, just go down to Hell and ask anybody there and they will tell you all about it.*

Before he left, John-de-Conqueror passed around iced water to everybody in Hell, and turned the furnace damper down a bit. He knew that he and his bride would be coming back to visit the folks one day, and he 'didn't like the house kept so hot like the Devil has been keeping it'. If he came back and found the Devil had turned it up again, he promised to tear down the whole job and put up an ice house in its place.

The tales of John-de-Conqueror have given rise to later opinions of Hell by black Americans, in which the inhabitants have taken over and put in shag rugs, indirect lighting and an open bar. Now there's always good music down there, altogether a completely different sort of place from where the white folk get sent. 🐾

parallelhells

# picturesque hell

## Hell Sells

The most entertaining whacky Hells are not in any religion, but in the Prado in Madrid, with its fine collection of Flemish paintings, in particular those by **Hieronymus Bosch** (1460–1516). Bosch's ultimate in wicked pleasure fantasies, the *Garden of Earthly Delights*, offers a healthy antidote to all those dark and dreary Last Judgements of the day, and

the background. Bosch's trippy Hells and his *Table of the Seven Deadly Sins* (set in a big eyeball, with warnings, 'Beware, Beware, God is Watching You!') acutely presage the anxiety and guilt of the coming age and were avidly collected by the bureaucratic and fanatically Catholic Philip II of Spain, and were the only light-hearted objects to decorate his sterile monastic death palace, El Escorial.

Hieronymus Bosch *The garden of earthly delights*

looks ahead to Dali and Hunter S. Thompson. His demons more often than not are winsome creatures, Humpty Dumpties, or deer, rabbits, pigs, birds and reptiles, or composites thereof, who have chats with the damned while administering interesting tortures in fun-house settings, while the satanic city smoulders in

Bosch's greatest follower in the Hell genre was **Pieter Bruegel the Elder** (1525–69), who was patronized by Cardinal Antoine Perrenot de Granville, advisor to Philip II, although his Hells are believed to have been satires of the Spanish control of the Netherlands. Bruegel's imps often seem derived from

Bosch's, humorous creatures from the wrong side of the looking glass. His sons, **Pieter the Younger** (1564–1638), and **Jan ('Velvet') Bruegel** (1568–1625), continued in their father's footsteps, producing innumerable infernal follies (Pieter the Younger was actually nicknamed 'Hell Bruegel'); all their works were snapped up by insatiable Spanish collectors. Their Hells, like carnivals, are

ing soul, but the work created a scandal as the artist took the liberty of not only stripping the damned, as tradition demanded, but the saints, too—even Jesus was starkers. A member of the Pope's administration, Biagio da Cesena, complained so much that the Paul ordered Michelangelo to cover them up. Michelangelo refused, and got back by painting Biagio's face on the fig-

Michelangelo *The Last Judgement*

liable to contain anyone or anything—anything goes.

The same century also saw the ultimate Italian Hell: **Michelangelo's** *Last Judgement*, frescoed from 1508–12 for Paul III in the Sistine Chapel. Like other Italian Hells, it's appropriately gloomy, with unforgettable images of an implacable Jesus and the despair-

ure of Minos. Biagio protested to the pope, who replied, 'Had the painter sent you to Purgatory, I would use my best efforts to get you released; but I exercise no influence in Hell; there you are beyond redemption.' Biagio's still there, but so are the loin draperies added after Michelangelo was safely dead.  ♣

parallel hells

> Mean blue fairies
> stuck they forks
> in me,
> Made me moan,
> and groan
> in misery
> Bessie Smith

## the mesopotamians and the egyptians

Hell's first documented colonists were dying/reviving vegetation gods and goddesses, who would pop down for a season and return with the corn, which they encouraged to grow from their experience in the soil. The first recorded visitor to 'the Great Below', in the 19th century BC, was the Mesopotamian goddess **Inanna** (or Ishtar, or Astarte, the 'storehouse of dates'). Inanna's stated intention in going to Hell was a social visit to her sister **Queen Ereshkigal**—the first known boss of the underworld was a woman.

The details on Hell under Ereshkigal are scanty, though she doesn't seem to be a very good housekeeper; there's dust everywhere. She's an even worse hostess: as the mighty Inanna makes her way down, Ereshkigal's minions make her strip off a piece of her finery (and implicitly her divine powers) at each gate, until, humiliatingly naked, Inanna at least meets Ereshkigal, and flies at her throat. But Ereshkigal is the mistress in her realm and hangs Inanna from a stake. After three days of infertility on earth, the other gods beg Ereshkigal to let Inanna go, but she does so only on condition that Inanna finds a hostage. Inanna seizes on her own boyfriend Dumuzi, and hands him over to Ereshkigal's demons. Dumuzi, however, gets a break from his bleak sentence when his mother and sister come looking for him, and

Plaque of Hell

his sister kindly agrees to stand in for half a year.

With gates and demons and a penchant for tortures, Ereshkigal's Hell is a dismal place, and the threat of it weighs heavily in the oldest discovered epic, the **story of Gilgamesh**. Its protagonist is the arrogant and violent King of Erech, whose thoughts are not turned from earthly matters until his bosom friend Enkidu suddenly dies. Heartbroken, Gilgamesh begs the gods to let him see his friend once more, and Enkidu's flitting shade dutifully returns to inform him that Hell is full of dirt and vermin. Everyone, with the exception of one lucky mortal named Utnapishtim, ends up there, and even the great Gilgamesh himself is doomed.

Horrified by the prospect, Gilgamesh makes a long journey to Utnapishtim to learn the secret of immortality and find the plant of eternal youth. But this is no sooner found than it is gobbled up by a snake, which thereafter had the ability to rejuvenate itself by shedding its old skin. The lesson of the tale is clear—we can't win.

The meticulous Egyptians tidied up the Underworld, drew the first maps, and set the precedents for law and order. The ritual formulae laid down in the *Book of the Dead* offered precise post-mortem instructions. There was to be a ride in a boat across the celestial river of the Milky Way where the deceased would be met by the dog-headed god Anubis, before being led to the sacrificed and resurrected god

history

Osiris for judgement. Osiris, it turns out, didn't really have much control over the verdict; after pleading their cases, the dead would have to give their hearts to Anubis, who would place them in the scales and weigh them against a feather from the headdress of Maat, the goddess of Truth. A good heart would sit in the balance, but a heart heavy with sin would sink, and a little monster named Ammit would eat it up in a flash.

Curiously enough, the good Egyptians' perils were not over. They would receive new bodies and be released into the Field of Rushes, a temporary but anarchic swampy Hell where crocodiles lurked and there was always the danger of putrifying or even dying all over again. Fortunately, the *Book of the Dead* also prescribed spells to get through these dangers before the dead could settle down to a blissful new life, enjoying the furniture, finery and toys left in their tombs.

Later rulers of the Dark Realm would sort out the gravity problem, but the Egyptians do deserve credit for establishing many of Hell's most enduring features, especially the trial of the soul, and the scales that weigh good and evil. Giving away new bodies after death was too good an idea to stay out of favour for long. Anubis, too, though the last dog to play an important role as a psychopomp, or conductor of souls, was only the first of many infernal canines.

## Zoroaster takes over
### and makes the underworld sheer Hell

The prophet Zoroaster, or Zarathustra, was one of the great innovators in religious affairs. Zoroastrianism held sway in central Asia until the Muslim conquests in the 7th century, and it still survives in India, where its adherants are called the Parsi ('Persians'). Zoroaster himself is a rather elusive character, born in Azerbaijan, or northern Persia, as early as the 18th century BC, or according to some, as late as the 7th century BC. At age 30, he received a vision from Ahura Mazda, the Wise Lord, who appointed him to preach the truth to the world.

Zaroaster inherited the Hell of the Mesopotamians and Egyptians but changed it significantly, by handing it over to **Ahriman**, the Evil Spirit, Lord of Darkness, Evil and Death, and his *daevas*, or devils. Ahriman is a key character, for according to Zarathustra, all of existence is to be explained by the cosmic, dualistic strife between bad Ahriman and good

dogs, but if the bad deeds predominate, the soul goes to Hell to be punished by the *daevas*. If good and bad are exactly equal, the soul goes to limbo-like **Hammistagan**.

Zarathustra also prophesied a last showdown between Ahura Mazda and Ahriman, a mighty battle that would bring with it the end of the world. A savior named **Soshyans**, Zarathustra's son, born of a virgin,

> Boldly firing all the other gods, Zarathustra gave the individual the power and freedom to choose between good and evil.

**Ahura Mazda**, Lord of Light and Order who lived up in Heaven with his seven angels. Boldly firing all the other gods, Zaroaster gave the individual the power and freedom to choose between good and evil. At death, the soul is judged by **Rashnu and Mithra**, who keep an account book listing all the good and bad deeds committed in life. If there are more good works than bad, the soul is escorted over a bridge to bliss by the fair **Daena** and her two guard

will harrow Hell and save all the souls there who repent; as the forces of Good and Light triumph Hell will be destroyed in a sea of molten metal and a new kingdom of God will appear on earth. Zoroastrianism not only had a powerful influence on the growth of monotheism in the Middle East, but its dualistic world view (in which good and evil have equal powers) would periodically bedevil Christianity, reappearing in the Manichaean and Cathar heresies.

# Hades:
## Hell in Classical Times—
### An In Place for Everybody
#### who is Anybody

The ancient Greeks, unlike the Egyptians, Jews or Zoroastrians, were content to leave the arrangement of Hell, or Hades, to poets, and rampant eschatological confusion is the rule. On one hand, there were the secret Eleusian mysteries, featuring the most potent dying/reviving vegetation deity in Greek myth: **Kore**, daughter of Demeter the Corn Goddess. Kore as a young girl was gathering flowers when Hades, the lord of the underworld, whisked her away to his dark realm, where she refused all food while her mother roamed the earth in search of her daughter, in her distress letting all the crops wither and die. Demeter reached Eleusis just as humanity was about to starve, when Zeus intervenes and a compromise is reached, allowing Kore to spend two thirds of the year on the surface of the earth; Hades has the right to keep her for the other third, because while down below she made the fatal mistake of nibbling seven pomegranate seeds.

Initiates into the secret Eleusinan Mysteries re-enacted the ritual and were said to be less fearful of death.

As Plutarch quotes the playwright Sophocles, 'Thrice blessed are those mortals who see these mysteries before departing to Hades; for they alone have true life there. All that is evil besets the rest.'

The 'evil' Sophocles referred to was the dreary Hades that awaited Greeks. Unlike Zoroastrian Hell, everyone ended up there, no matter whether they were naughty or nice. Hesiod laid Hades' foundations in the *Theogony* in the 8th century BC: Erebus, the upper zone of Hades, and Tartarus, the lower zone, both of which emerged at the same time as Night and Earth. Tartarus had a great pit or Abyss, ruled by the Infernal couple Hades and Kore, who had very quickly adapted to her role down below and adopted the name Persephone, which means 'the Bringer of Destruction'.

Homer set a number of infernal precedents in his *Odyssey* when the witch Circe advises Odysseus to visit Hades to seek advice from the dead prophet Tiresias. **Odysseus** sails north to the Grove of Persephone and sacrifices a black ram and ewe, so that their blood ran into a trough. This drew the dead out from a cavern; as the ancient philosopher Heraclitus later explained, the only sense the shades retained was that of smell. By drinking the blood, the rustling, flitting ghosts briefly regain the power of speech, although only that; when Odysseus attempts to embrace his mother, he hugs only air.

For the Greeks this was discomfiting. Homeric warrior aristocracy owed all its happiness to a strong healthy body and couldn't imagine anything worse than a wraithlike, insubstantial existence in the afterlife: the dead hero **Achilles** tells exceptions to the rule: these form our first accounts of customized torments for big sinners. Ixion, who attempted to rape Hera, Zeus' wife, was tied to a fiery wheel; Tityus, the Titan who dared to attack Leto, the mother of Apollo and Artemis, was stretched out across a vast area, and pinned down while vultures eternally ate his liver; Tantalus, who cooked up his son to serve the gods, was tantalized by hunger and thirst; Sisyphus, who presumed to meddle in divine

Tantalus.       Sisyphus.       Ixion.

...inhabitants of later Hells might think they were getting off lightly.

Odysseus that he'd rather be a farm labourer working for a poor man than king of all the tired dead. Later visitors to Greek and Roman Hades had to listen to similar griping; inhabitants of later Hells might think they were getting off lightly.

Nearly all the punishments administered by the Greek gods were meted out in this life and not the next, but Odysseus is witness to a few famous affairs by giving away the secret of one of Zeus' many intrigues, was condemned to push a boulder up a hill that would always roll back just before reaching the top. We also meet Minos, the legendary king of Crete and son of Zeus, who serves as Hell's judge, a position he would keep for centuries.

Although Odysseus doesn't descend into Hades for a closer look, a handful

of other Greeks do. The Egyptian Milky Way is replaced by the river Styx ('Despised') and its tributaries: Cocytus ('Wailing'), Acheron ('Sorrow') Phlegethon ('Burning'), and Lethe ('Forgetfulness'). Charon, the infernal

assigned the **abyss of Tartarus** to keep company with the Cyclops, the Titans and others who dared to rebel against the gods. The not-so-bad went to the **Fields of Asphodel**, to flit about rather gloomily, while the virtuous and hero-

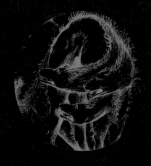

## The worldly Greeks were the first not to treat Hell altogether seriously

gondolier, ferries souls over the Styx for two *obols*. The three-headed dog Cerberus guards the gate, and there are other unpleasantries: Medusa, the Furies, and the *keres*, the death spirits with wings, one for each soul, who functioned like negative guardian angels. By the 5th century BC, the Greeks introduced Zoroastrian or Egyptian ideas about posthumous reckonings, and appointed three judges in Hades: Rhadamanthys (Minos' brother) who judged Asians, Aeacus (Minos' enemy) in charge of Europeans, and Minos, the legendary king of Crete, who ran the court of appeals. The truly wicked were

ic got the **Elysian Fields**, where they could practise sport or play draughts, or play the lyre, and feast on the scent of barbeque, thanks to Elysian sacrifices on earth.

The worldly Greeks were the first not to treat Hell altogether seriously and under their tenure the first living mortals were permitted to descend for a peek. **Theseus**, the king of Athens, was persuaded by his friend Peirithoos to help him abduct the fair **Helen**, still a little girl at the time but fated to become the most beautiful woman in the world. When they query the oracle at Delphi for advice, the reply comes: 'Why not abduct

Persephone herself?' Perithoos was dumb enough to take the scoffing oracle seriously, and Theseus was dumb enough to go along. They entered Hades through the cave of Taenarus, the southernmost tip of the Mani peninsula in the Peloponnese. Grim Hades welcomed them, and knowing they were after his better half, asked them to have a seat on the Chair of Forgetfulness, nipped by serpents and Cerberus and taunted by Hades for their gullibility.

Fortunately, before setting out, Theseus had acted as sponsor to the greatest Greek hero of them all,

Baron Antoine Jean Gros *Hercules and Diomedes*

**Heracles** (Roman Hercules), at the mysteries of Eleusis, in preparation for his Eleventh Labour: to fetch Cerberus from Hades. Heracles descended through the cave of Taenarus, and burst into Hades, terrifying all the inhabitants. Finding his old sponsor Theseus stuck to the chair, he yanked him up so abruptly that most of his skin stayed on the seat, and he was about to rescue Peirithoos, too, but Hades stepped in and forbade him, and for all anyone knows he's still there. Heracles then seized Hades' three-headed dog and dragged him and Theseus out of Hell; King Eurystheus, for whom Heracles had to preform his Labours, took one look at Cerberus and hid trembling in a giant jar until Heracles sent him back to Hades.

Heracles was the only man to willingly return to Hades. A friend of his, **King Admetus**, had been offered a deal by the Grim Reaper: if he could find a volunteer to die in his place, his life would be spared. When all, even Admetus' elderly parents, refused to take his place, his wife Alcestis took poison. Heracles, indignant, went back to Hades to fetch Alcestis, which Persephone allowed, just this once, because she agreed that it wasn't right for a woman to die for her husband: the story formed the basis of Euripides' play *Alcestis*. However, when Euripides himself died and went to Hades in 405 BC, he was followed (according to Aristophanes' comedy *The Frogs*) by **Dionysos**, the god of wine and theatre, and his wise-cracking servant Xanthias. Complaining that Greece no longer

had any poets, Dionysos wanted to bring Euripides back to Athens, and hoping to make his visit to Hades easier, he disguised himself as Heracles, with lion pelt and club. Of course, just the opposite happened, as everyone in Hell was ready to thump him in revenge for his previous two visits; Dionysos barely escaped the Hellhounds of Cocytus, the hundred-headed Asp, the Tartesian Lamprey, and the Tithrasian Gorgons. In Aristophanes' Hades, croaking frogs have filled the once fearsome Styx, and some fun is had at the expense of a band of mystics from Eleusis tiptoeing through the tulips. The play ends with an infernal poetic contest, and when Aeschylus is declared the victor, Dionysos brings him back to earth.

## Orphic Hell: the Original Millennial Recycling Programme

The most important visitor to Greek Hades was the famous musician/poet from Thrace, **Orpheus**. When his beloved wife Eurydice died from a snakebite, Orpheus went down and sang so sweetly and sadly before Hades and Persephone that they took pity on him and permitted Eurydice to follow Orpheus to earth, as long as he didn't look at her until they reached the surface. He couldn't wait, and looked, and lost her.

The hexameter 'Verses of Orpheus', well known in the ancient world, were the scriptures for a rather mysterious sect called the Orphics. Their Hades was pretty much the Greek standard, but with a difference–it was only a way station. The Orphics explained why with another myth: the baby god Dionysos was lured away with toys by Zeus' archenemies, the giant Titans, who slew him, cooked him, and ate him before Zeus found out and blasted them to ashes with a thunderbolt. Athena managed to save Dionysos' heart, allowing him to be reborn, while the human race sprang from the ashes of the god and the Titans. Hence humans have two aspects, one divine and the other material, or 'Titanic', heavy and prone to sink into wickedness, a concept that would grow like Topsy into the Doctrine of Original Sin.

The task of the immortal Dionysian soul was to cleanse away all traces of Titanic nature by living through 'a weary cycle' of incarnations, until sufficiently purified to become a god once more and live in eternal bliss. At death, a soul would be judged, and if the verdict was good, it would enjoy the delights of the Elysian Fields; if bad, there were suitable punishments in Hades. After a thousand years, the soul would drink the waters of forgetfulness from the fountain Lethe, and return to earth either as a human or animal (the Orphics were vegetarians). A run of the mill soul had to repeat the thousand-year cycle ten times, but by initiation and participation in certain rites, and by abstemious, pure and morally upright living, a soul could escape the weary cycle. If a soul was so hardened in evil that the judges of Hades reckoned no amount of reincarnating could possibly improve it, it was sent to eternal punishment in Tartarus, side by side with Sisyphos and Tantalos.

The Orphic belief in a divine soul ran counter to much of classical Greek thought, which advised moderation and avoiding the hubris of imitating the gods. Equally strange was the idea of a personal religion dedicated to salvation of the individual soul. Pythagoras, Plato and Empedocles were influenced by Orphic writings; but they also got

Jan the Elder Brueghel *Orpheus and Persephone*

into the hands of quacks (mocked by Plato in *The Republic*) who are roundly condemned for offering everlasting life like a bribe and threatening Hell fire to the unrepentant, so that people would think only of their personal future, and not seek goodness for its own sake.

↓

## A Tour of Roman Hell

Sticklers for form, the Romans took the Greek myths as they found them, only changing names to those of their own Latin deities. Persephone became Proserpina and Hades, Pluto, but also *Dives Pater* 'Father Wealthy Man' or Dis for short.

The Romans were great builders and organizers, and in the *Aeneid* (30–19 BC), Virgil sorts out Hell, building features and landscapes there that would endure for centuries in the Hells of the Latin fathers of the Church, especially Augustine. In the sixth book of the *Aeniad*, Virgil's hero **Aeneas**, a Trojan prince looking for a new homeland after the fall of Troy, lands at Cumae on the Bay of Naples. Aeneas asks advice of the **Cumaean Sibyl** in her cave (rediscovered by accident in 1932; this cave near Naples can be visited today). Aeneas wants to go to Hell. Since the death of his father Anchises, Aeneas says, his spirit has haunted his dreams, asking him to visit the realm of dead. After all, one of the main entrances, on the shore of Lake Avernus, is right there by Cumae. The Sibyl tells him that if he wants to make a return trip, he must first pluck the Golden Bough from the sacred grove as a gift for Proserpina.

Virgil's hero was the first to have the advantage of an experienced guide in the Sybil, who takes him step by step through the infernal regions. As in the *Odyssey*, entry hinges on a sacrifice of black animals to Pluto, Proserpina and Hecate, the Witch Queen of the Night. The hag eventually appears, and leads the way inside the jaws of Hell, where they find Cares and

Andrea del Castagno *The Cuman Sibyl*

Sorrows, Age, Diseases, Famine, Toils, Death, and Death's half-brother, Sleep. Aeneas makes ready to fight but the Sibyl dismisses them all as

dreams from the cave of Sleep. Next the Sibyl and Aeneas meet Charon, 'a sordid god', a grouchy, greasy old slob who refuses to transport any more mortals in his ferry, until the Sibyl shows him the Golden Bough.

Once across the murky Styx, the Sibyl tosses a drugged honeycake to Cerberus, and when the hound keels over the two pass into Hell proper, where they find newborn babies and people unjustly put to death; Minos the judge is there, although instead of scales to separate the just from the wicked, he rolls 'blended' balls in an urn, rather like the lottery on TV. Next Aeneas finds the 'foolish' people who threw away their souls: the suicides, and in the Mournful Fields, lovers who *'pining with desire. Lament too late their unextinguish'd fire'*.

These souls all belong to women who died from unhappy loves; here Aeneas finds his lover Dido, the Queen of Carthage who killed herself when he abandoned her. Virgil, like Dante, felt sorry for victims of passion. Next Aeneas meets his old war buddies from Troy, who have a long moan about their deaths in the Homeric manner until the Sibyl can't take anymore and hastens Aeneas on. As in Orphic Hell, the road forks, the left branch leading to Tartarus and

to separate the just from the wicked, he rolls 'blended' balls in an urn, rather like the lottery on TV

punishment, and the right to Pluto's golden palace. They take the right, but on the way Aeneas has a look and finds a lofty tower full of noise, fire and stench. Virgil's great contributions to the Hellscape may have been inspired by local geography, all volcanic: Cumae is near the firey Phlegraean Fields, of sulphurous gas vents and overheated fumeroles, while Avernus, a crater lake, was famous for its sulphuric vapours. But there's more. Aeneas hears awful sounds no Greek ever heard in Hades, of whips, chains and roaring bellows, and the Sibyl tells him how Tartarus works. The vengeful gods have set up Rhadamanthus to judge each crime. Afterwards, the Furies seize the guilty ghost, and the gate opens of its own accord, revealing the Hell Mouth, 'whose jaws with iron teeth severely grin'. Down in the pit are the

celebrities that Odysseus saw, and more: misers, cheaters, adulterers, deserters, traitors, and those guilty of incest. And more, too horrible for the Sibyl to tell.

The Sibyl leads Aeneas instead to Pluto's palace, where the Golden Bough grants them access to the Elysian Fields, a land of green meadows, with its own suns and stars, where they find the happy souls, including Orpheus. Here Aeneas finds his father **Anchises**, who explains Orphism to him in some detail. The doctrine of transmigration comes in handy here, allowing Anchises to introduce, in the queue of souls waiting to drink the soporific waters of Forgetfulness, Aeneas' descendants-to-be, the kings and heroes of Rome; the scene allows Virgil to flatter his patron and friend, Augustus. A tour of the Elysian Fields follows, and ends at the two gates of Sleep; one of transparent horn, through which true visions pass, and another polished ivory, through which pass 'deluding lies'. Anchises quickly takes his leave through the gate of delusion. Was it a small hint that Virgil didn't mean all that he said?

One of Rome's secret weapons was getting other people's gods to defect to their side, by promising them better and bigger temples and sacrifices. **Mithra**, was brought back from Persia in the late 1st century BC and enjoyed immensely popularity for five centuries, especially in Roman military circles. Mithra (Mitra-Varuna) was an Indo-Persian god, worshipped at least as early as 1400 BC as the Lord of Heavenly Light, protector of truth. He was far too popular for Zoroaster to dismiss him in his reforms of Persian polytheism, and he made Mithra the special son of the Lord of Light and judge of the dead.

Mithraism was a mystery cult, with seven degrees of initiation under the protection of the seven planets, allowing the soul to reverse its descent in the material world, the Mithraic equivalent of Hell. Although persecuted out of existence by the Christians in the 4th century, Mithraism gave the Church its Seven Deadly Sins—originally the seven errors a soul could fall into during initiation. The Mithraic holy father's mitre, ring, and shepherd's staff became the outfit and title of the Christian bishop. Mithras' birthday,

*Mithra sacrificing the Bull with Sol and Luna*

25 December, became Christ's. Our honeymoons come from the Mithraic purification with honey while an initiate was under the protection of the Moon, from the Persian belief that the moon was the source of honey.

## Jewish Sheol and Gehenna

Monotheistic by the time of Moses (13th century BC), Judaism, of all the Middle Eastern religions, was the one least subject to influence from its pantheistic neighbours. Also, unlike

later monotheists, the focus of Judaism is on this world rather than the next, stressing conduct rather than doctrinal correctness. Jews have always had a measure of latitude in eschatalogical concerns, notably about the coming of the Messiah and the afterlife. They were also remarkably uninterested in Hell.

Although often translated as 'Hell' in English, *Sheol* ('sunk in, hollow') in the Hebrew Bible/Old Testament is a neutral term for the grave. *Gehenna*, the other word translated as 'Hell', means the 'valley of the sons of Hinnom'. Nobody remembers whom Hinnom might have been, but his sons' valley is located south of Jerusalem (at modern Wadi er-rababi). In ancient times, it saw the nasty worship of Moloch with its human sacrifices. Defiled by Josias (IV Kings, xxiii, 10) and cursed by Jeremiah, *Gehenna* was a rubbish heap, where a fire was kept alight to burn garbage and the bodies of dead animals and criminals.

In later writings, however, especially in Isaiah (3rd or 4th century BC) there are hints of the resurrection of the body and bad news for people who fail to keep faith with Yahweh. 'The dead men shall live, together with my dead body shall they arise. Awake and sing, ye that dwell in dust: for their dew is as the dew of herbs, and the earth shall cast out the dead' (Isaiah 26:19). Such references are dismissed as evidence of Zoroastrian influence on the Jews during the Babylonian Captivity (587–536 BC), but whatever the origin, eschatology remained a favourite obsession with the Pharisees (a small intellectual élite, their name comes from the Hebrew 'perusim' meaning 'those who have been set apart'.

As opposed to their rival sect, the proud, aristocratic and conservative Sadducees, the Pharisees posited a resurrection of the dead, in a complex hierarchy of angels, and in a Hell of eternal punishment for those who disobeyed the *Ten Commandments*. And their beliefs prevailed during a crucial moment: it was the Pharisees who held the Jews together after the destruction of the Temple by the Romans in AD 70 and into the 2nd century. Josephus, the great 1st-century AD historian, was a Pharisee, and so was Saul of Tarsus, before he became St Paul.

The eternal Hell of the Pharisees was not nice, and is best described in the 2nd-century BC *Book of Enoch*, one of the most widely read of the pseudepigrapha, a 'book with a false title,' the authors of which gave them the names of persons from earlier epochs to enhance their authority. Enoch, or whoever was using his name, saw:

> a deep abyss, with columns of Heavenly fire, and among them I saw columns of fire fall, which were beyond measure alike towards the height and towards the depth. And beyond that abyss I saw a place which had no firmament of the Heaven above, and no firmly founded earth beneath it: there was no water upon it, and no birds, but it was a waste and horrible place.

Although Jesus told his apostles to beware of the Pharisees and called them 'whitewashed tombs' in Matthew 23:27, he shared many of their beliefs, including the physical resurrection of the dead. But whether or not he preached their fiery eternal Hell is still a subject of debate.

## Lucifer Takes a Stand, and Has a Nasty Fall

> It is Lucifer, Son of Mystery
> And since God suffers him to be,
> He, too, is God's minister
> And labors for some good
> By us not understood.
>
> Longfellow

Monotheistic religions have found it tough going explaining why evil exists in a divinely created world, and there is some speculation that Satan ('the adversary' in Hebrew) wasn't so much created by God but by the writers of the Old Testament, to take the rap for Yahweh's sadistic dirty work: tempting Eve, tormenting Job, killing off the first born in Egypt, and so on. Even Satan's role in tempting Judas to betray Jesus would seem to be essential in the divinely ordained script of the Passion. Somebody had to do it. Hissing at him seems like hissing at the villain in a melodrama.

Satan the fallen angel first appears in Isaiah's fulminations at the King of Babylon: *'How art thou fallen from Heaven, O Lucifer, son of the morning! How you are cut down to the ground you who laid the nations low! You said in your heart 'I will ascend to Heaven, Above the stars of God I will set my throne on high.'* And in Ezekiel 28:12–23, *'Thou art the annointed cherub that covereth; and I have set thee so: thou wast on the holy mountain of God: thou hast walked up and down in the stones of fire. Thou wast perfect in thy ways from the day thou wast created till iniquity was found in thee...'* Lucifer, 'Bearer of Light' is the translation of the Hebrew *Helel ben Shahar*, 'Bright Son of the Morning'. Jesus identifies him with Satan in Luke 10:18: *'I beheld Satan as lightning fall from Heaven,'* and the general theory seems to be that he changed his name when he changed address.

The *Haggadah*, a collection of Jewish legends written down in the 4th century BC, fills in the details: Lucifer was the most beautiful of all God's creatures, the cream of the seraphim, angels so high and mighty they possessed six wings. Rather than beautiful, this makes Lucifer sound like an exotic insect: artists painstakingly trying to depict seraphim as described often end up just giving them a head with six multicoloured wings folded around it. Whatever he looked like, Lucifer became envious of God's new creation, or of Adam. In other versions, he wanted to become God himself, and from his envy and pride Sin was born. He dared to sit in the throne of God, and attracted a third of the Heavenly host to his cause. Archangel Michael, Heaven's generalissimo, led the loyal angels in a mighty battle against the rebels; they are defeated, and God hurls them like falling stars down to Hell, where they were chained, waiting to be judged.

That Lucifer 'the Bearer of Light' rebelled against the tyrannical Yahweh of the Old Testament has seemed quite reasonable to many people: the thinking man's angel, knowing he could never have any intellectual freedom up in totalitarian Heaven, may not have been fired. Perhaps he just resigned.

# Christian Hell:
## early ambiguities

As can be seen, a vast underground edifice was already in place when the early Christians staked their claim to Hell and began to argue about the wallpaper. That a religion based on love and redemption felt obliged to maintain a cellar full of torture instruments and blazing furnaces may seem odd, and the first few centuries witnessed a great deal of arguing and excommunicating over the issue.

Christianity's first missionary and theologian, Paul, whose writings are the oldest in the New Testament, taught that 'the wages of sin is death', recalling the annihilation theory of the Egyptians. When writing to the decadent Corinthians and others, he listed all the unrepentent sinners that would be excluded from the Kingdom of God (thieves, adulterers, idolaters, and people who indulge in the seven deadlies), but he never wrote that exclusion meant a ticket to Hell.

The four canonical gospels were penned later. Mark, written around the year 70, is the earliest, and here Jesus mentions Hell once (9:43–48)

*If thy hand offend thee, cut it off: it is better for thee to enter into life maimed than having two hands to go into Hell, into the fire that shall*

*never be quenched: Where their worm dieth not and the fire is not quenched. And if thy foot offend thee, cut it off...*

The worm that dieth not and the unquenchable fire refers to Isaiah 66:24, but this Hell prevention technique never caught the popular fancy as much as the story in Luke of Dives and Lazarus. The Gospels of Mark and Luke are commonly believed to be been based on a lost common source (known as 'Q') but Luke, the companion of St Paul, is the only one to mention Jesus' parable of wealthy Dives at his table and the ragged beggar Lazarus, waiting for scraps that never come. Lazarus gets his reward 'in the bosom of Abraham' while stingy Dives goes into the fire of Hades. He asks Abraham to send Lazarus over with a drink of water, but Abraham refuses, telling Dives that he has already enjoyed 'his good things', and they are separated by an unbridgeable gap.

Taken literally (as it was, like no other parable in the Bible) the presence of Abraham in bliss made the invention of a benign Limbo necessary for the Patriarchs of the Old Testament. It also put Heaven and

Hell within speaking distance. Artists would depict Abraham with his long beard sitting among the elect looking down into Hell, sometimes with a mirror image (as in the mosaics of Torcello cathedral in Venice) of Satan holding his son the Antichrist on his lap.

John, the third-oldest gospel, makes no reference to Hell, but Matthew, the last to be written, certainly makes up for it. Matthew is generally dated around the year 80, in spite of its claims to be by one of Jesus' disciples. The persecutions of the Christians had already begun (by Emperor Nero in the year 64) and Matthew offers a stern admonition to keep the faith, '*Whomever shall deny me before men, him will I also deny before my Father who is in Heaven*' (10:33). Over and over again in Matthew one finds Jesus' parables, similar to the other gospels, but this time with threats of punishment attached for offenders, which Matthew himself tacked on for emphasis. And these became the prime Gospel references to the existence of Hell.

But exactly what kind of Hell was it? Any mention of everlasting torments for unrepentant sinners and unbelievers was omitted from the earliest documents pertaining to sin and redemption, the *Teaching of the Twelve Apostles* (120–160 AD), and from the *Apostles' Creed*, which took its shape between 250 and 350. Rather than gain converts by threats, the new religion faced its tormentors and scoffers by emphasizing eternal life. Tombs in the catacombs were decorated with hopeful symbols such as fish (the name in capital Greek letters was the code for Christ), anchors, harps, palms, and crowns; the earliest certain Latin cross only appears in 451, on the tomb of the Empress Galla Placidia in Ravenna.

Yet while some preached sweetness and light, the hellfire element was always just around the corner. One of the most influential writers, Tertullian of Africa (c. 160–230) gleefully wrote that he could hardly wait until the end of the world, when he could laugh at all the sinners frying in Hell. Philosophers flambéed, fallen kings, persecuting governors 'melting in flames fiercer than those they kindled for brave Christians,' poets, actors, even athletes, cartwheeling in flames 'These are things of greater delight, I believe,' drooled Tertullian, 'than a circus, both kinds of theatre, and any kinds of stadium.'

## Alexandrian Universalism: Hell as a Cleanser

*UNIVERSALIST, n. One who forgoes the advantage of a Hell for persons of another faith.*

The Devil's Dictionary

The first men to look at Christianity philosophically were **Clement of Alexandria** (then 'more Greek than Athens') and his follower **Origen**. The Greek fathers of the Church never found Hell as attractive as Tertullian and the Latins; for a while they gave the Latins a run for their money.

Clement of Alexandria (150–220) came to Christianity steeped in Greek philosophy, especially Plato. Clement stated that God was nothing but good, though like the fallen angels our souls have fallen away from him. But we possess a spark of immortal divinity that would ultimately purify us and elevate us to a higher life; virtue would accelerate, and sin impede our upward progress. On Hell, Clement wrote that, 'Punishment is, in its operation, like medicine; it dissolves the hard heart, purges away the filth of uncleanness, and reduces the swellings of pride and haughtiness... restoring its sub-ject to a sound and healthful state.'

Clement's disciple, Origen, born in 185, went even further. Defending the philosopher Celsus's criticism that the Christian God was 'a baker' for frying people in flames. Origen explained that 'Gehenna was a purifying fire' not material fire but spiritual remorse that would eventually result in reformation, salvation and glorifi-cation of all spirits, even the fallen angels and Satan himself. For eternity, Origen reasoned, was certainly long enough for even the most wicked soul to improve, even after death.

Both Clement and Origen wrote in Greek, using the same vocabulary as the original Gospels. Part of Origen's argument against the eternity of Hell was based on the use of Greek words in the text. *Aionan* ('for ages', eons, but not forever) is used when describing the punishment for sins, rather than *aidon* ('everlasting'). When talking about punishment in Hell, the word Jesus used was translated *kolasin*, chastisement, with the meaning to improve, rather than *timoria*, punishment in a retributive way.

The Latinists, especially Tertullian and Augustine, never made the distinction. They also had the Roman urge to adhere strictly to formalities and authority. Eternal Hell triumphed at last in 543, when the Synod of Constantinople stated:

> *If anyone shall say or think that there is a time limit to the torment of demons and ungodly persons, or that there will ever be an end to it, or that they will ever be pardoned or made whole again, then let him be excommunicated.*

Origen, whose death has been called 'the real end of free Christianity and, in particular, of free intellectual theology' was duly excommunicated, and re-excommunicated just to make sure. His surviving books were burned. His teacher, Clement, was struck off the list of saints by Benedict XIV in the 18th century. ◖

## The Harrowing of Hell—
### The Great One-Off
### Get-Out-of-Jail-Free Card

The first and most popular Christian Hell was little worse than a dingy prison with a big crack running through it, with a broken gate and few inhabitants. After all, the *Apostles' Creed* reads, 'He descended into Hell [i.e. Hades]; The third day he rose again from the dead...' The New Testament source, *1 Peter 3:18, 19*, even explains what Jesus got up to down there, '*he went and preached unto the spirits in prison...*' So Christ went to Hell and proclaimed the Gospel to the dead! The Old Testament foretells the harrowing in Psalm 102:19, and 20 Isaiah 9:2, and at the time a Jewish story, the *Testament of the Twelve Patriarchs* (*c.* 100 BC), was making the rounds, starring the future Messiah who liberates Hells' captives.

What was to be, for many early and medieval Christians, one of the most stirring moments in the whole Passion cycle, is related in the colourful Gospel of Nicodemus (sometimes known as the Acts of Pilate) which appeared in the late 2nd century AD. In it, two sons of the priest Simeon are resurrected for three days at the same time as Jesus, in order to write a report on the big doings in Hell. Satan, 'the prince and captain of death', warns Beelzebub, the prince of Hell, that Jesus of Nazareth is coming. Beelzebub doesn't like the sound of this: Jesus is a troublemaker, who has been curing lepers, exorcising

demons, and raising people from the dead, but Satan assures him that Jesus is only 'a man afraid of death'. Beelzebub warns, however, 'When therefore he said he was afraid of death, he designed to ensnare you, and it will be unhappy to you for everlasting ages.'

Beelzebub got it right, for while he and Satan quibble Jesus breaks down the door, illuminating dark old Hell, breaking the fetters, trampling Death underfoot, and Beelzebub complains bitterly to Satan, 'He has broken down our prisons from top to bottom, dismissed all the captives, released all who were bound, and all who formerly were accustomed to groan under the weight of their torments have now insulted us.'

> *Then Jesus stretched forth his hand and said, Come to me, all you my saints, who were created in my image, who were condemned by the tree of forbidden fruit, and by the devil and death; Live now by the wood of my cross; the devil, the prince of this world, is overcome, and death is conquered.*

The idea that Jesus completely emptied Hell was prevalent in Augustine's day because he listed it amongst the heresies (number 79) for suggesting that Hell could have any limits and that somehow all the pagans who lived before Christ could be let off the hook. By the 9th century, the harrowing was officially limited to the Hebrew patriarchs.

It was in England that Nicodemus knew its greatest popularity. The Old/Middle English word harrowing first occurs in Aelfric's homilies, in about 1000, but the descent into Hell is recounted much earlier, in the Old English poems connected with Caedmon and Cynewulf.

## Last Judgements:
### Judiciary Teething Problems

Another problem facing the early Church was not only deciding who went to Hell for how long, but when. Zoroaster was the first to preach the idea that the world will end with a big bang, and a similar Day of Wrath is often promised in the Old Testament. Early Christians certainly thought the end was nigh. In Matthew's *Sermon on the Mount*, Jesus warns that the apocalypse, the time of false Christs, was at hand, '*This generation shall not pass till all these things be fulfilled. But of that day and hour knoweth no man, no, not the angels in Heaven, but my Father only.*'

In the first few centuries there was more than one 'Revelation' and

'Apocalypse' kicking around (*see below*). The one that made it into the canon, traditionally written in the year 95, only made it because it was erroneously believed to have been penned by Jesus' disciple John, rather than another John, 'of Patmos'. The end of the world, according to Patmos John, has to await the coming of the Antichrist, the son of Satan, murkily identified with Beast 666. After Armageddon, the Antichrist and

and references in the Gospel to the Good Thief, who would see Jesus in paradise that very day, and the afore-mentioned Harrowing of Hell argued for not one but two Judgements, as in Islam: particular (right after death) and universal. So like OJ Simpson we can expect two trials, though the verdict will remain the same both times. The Church defined the two degrees of torments: first, the *poena damni*, or pain of loss, total divorce of the soul

> ## So like OJ Simpson we can expect two trials, though the verdict will remain the same both times.

living unbelievers will be consumed in a 'lake that burns with fire and brimstone' (Rev. 21:8), along with Satan, Death, Hades itself, and all the wicked, purifying the world before the advent of the New Jerusalem.

As time went on, however, this promised Day of Wrath refused to dawn, and people began to ask: so what happened to the dead in the interval? The earliest Christians called necropoli cemeteries ('places of sleep', in Greek), but human nature

from God, causing immeasurable anguish and depression. The elect got to cool their heels in a relaxing wait-ing room (the *refrigerium*, in Augustine), at least until Purgatory was invented. After the Last Judgement, however, a second pun-ishment awaits the despairing souls; the *poena sensus*, or pain of sense, in an environmentally correct Hellfire that burns with a continually renewed supply of fuel.

# Pick a Number, Any Number

*Here is wisdom. He who has understanding, let him calculate the number of the beast, for it is the number of a man; and its number is six hundred and sixty-six.*

Revelations, 13:18

666: maladjusted teenagers scrawl it on the covers of their school books, and then grow up to be fundamentalist preachers who use it to prove that the Antichrist is the Coming Russian Dictator, or the Likely Democratic Presidential Candidate. A dissenting minority made much of the six letters in the names Ronald Wilson Reagan.

Occultists and Biblical scholars alike have been wracking their brains about this ever since St John wrote the book, without much success. A common guess is that the answer lies in the Hebrew *Kabbala*, where letters have numerical equivalents useful in conjuring and finding hidden connections. 666 is supposed to be the sum of the letters in the name *Nero Caesar*. That's a bit contrived, but it's very close. We just happen to know the answer, and we are going to tell you. We only wish it were less complicated and more infernally dramatic.

**Magic squares** have fascinated mystics and mathematicians for a long time; Pythagoras himself is said to have invented them. You'll remember that a magic square is an arrangement of numbers where each column adds up to the same sum, vertically, horizontally, and even diagonally. They come in all sizes, and the mystics long ago got the habit of associating each of them with one of the seven planetary spheres. The sphere of the sun was given the 6 by 6 square, a very complex magic square indeed.

Each of the columns adds up to 111 (111x6=666), and the sum of all the numbers in the square (the integers 1 to 36) is 666.

| 6 | 32 | 3 | 34 | 35 | 1 |
|---|----|---|----|----|---|
| 7 | 11 | 27 | 28 | 8 | 30 |
| 19 | 14 | 16 | 15 | 23 | 24 |
| 18 | 20 | 22 | 21 | 17 | 13 |
| 25 | 29 | 10 | 9 | 26 | 12 |
| 36 | 5 | 33 | 4 | 2 | 31 |

What does the sun have to do with it? Ever since the beginnings of monotheism in Egypt, there was a tendency to associate the One God with the sun, and the Romans after Augustus cleverly appropriated the symbolism to the emperor-worship that was the foundation of their state. The cult of the Emperor was the cult of *Sol Invictus*, the Unconquerable Sun (whose birthday incidentally was at the winter solstice, later taken over by the Christians as Christmas). In the Roman Empire, you could believe in any god you liked as long as you also rendered unto Caesar by sacrificing to the Emperor; not to do so was treason. To the hard-headed Christians, this was abomination. They refused, and got fried for it. Modern-day preachers can make whatever they like out of the *Book of Revelations*. To any educated Christian of John's time, however, there would be no doubt who the Antichrist really was, or where he resided. The seat of evil on earth was Rome, and the Beast was an oppressive tyrant and a false sun-god rolled into one.

## Alternative Apocalypses:
### Sexploitation and
### Diminishing Returns

The Church has always welcomed contributions, not only to its operating fund but to Hell; decorative details, and annexes could be added, as long as they were nasty enough. Some of the apocalypses left out of the Bible were so good at it that their Hell projects remained in place for centuries. In the *Apocalyspe of Peter* (mid 2nd century), a work once as popular as John of Patmos', pagans and persecuters of Christians are singled out for special mistreatment, as are sexual sinners. Punishments are meted out by 'angels', hanging blasphemers by their tongues over an open flame and adultresses by their hair above boiling mire. Murderers get a 'strait place full of evil, creeping things'. Women and their children born out of wedlock wallow up to their necks in a lake of stench; persecuters of the righteous have their entrails devoured by sleepless worms. The uncharitable rich were clad in filthy rags, rolling about 'on gravel-stones sharper than swords or any spit, heated with fire.' Usurers stand in a lake full of pus, blood and boiling mire; homosexuals are cast

over precipices, over and over again. And those who forsook God are 'roasted as in a pan.' As Alice Turner points out in her excellent *History of Hell*, such scenes were 'a form of self-righteous pornography' that would become one of Christianity's major contributions to Hell.

What's intriguing about most early apocalypses is that they often offer hope of release or at least a holiday from Hell, thanks to the intercession of the person having the vision. After taking in the horrors, Peter appeals to Christ to have pity on these sinners, only to be told by Jesus that it was secret, but *'because of them that have believed in me that I am come. It is also because of them that have believed in me, that, at their word, I shall have pity on men'*. The Sibylline Oracles, from the same period, even more explicitly predicted a similar final judgement of a merciful God, who would grant the righteous the boon of saving all men from 'the everlasting flame and remove them else whither, sending them for the sake of his people unto another life eternal and immortal, in the Elysian plain'. The later *Apocalypse of Paul* proposes even worse tortures laid on by dark angels under Tartaruchus, the personification of Greek Tartarus. Paul too begs Jesus

for mercy, and Jesus scolds him, but then grants sinners a 24-hour break every Easter.

The Virgin does somewhat better in the dreary but very popular 5th-century *Apocalypse of Mary*. Torments are described for the usual sinners, as well as some seemingly picayune new ones: people who failed to rise at the entry of a priest, and widows of priests who married again. The Virgin appeals to all the saints to intercede with her for the sinful Christians (no hope for the Jews, sorry). At last Jesus appears, and grants his mother the days of Pentecost as a season of rest to the lost—the precedent of the Blessed Virgin's present role as the Queen of Purgatory.

The *Revelation of Esdras* combines a preview of the Last Judgement and a tour of Heaven and Tartarus. Esdras finds Herod on a fiery throne; 'old men who would not listen' have burning pivots turning in their ears, a man guilty of incest hangs by the eyelids, a woman who drowned her children hangs with four wild beasts sucking her breasts. Throughout, Esdras begs God to have mercy on these sinners, and declares: *'Lord, it is good for man not to have been born.'* But God fails to make a convincing reply; it seems to be true.

For by the 4th century, God, the Father of the Christians, has begun to backslide into the dreadful Old Testament Yahweh: implacable, stern and vicious. People turned to Jesus to appease his Father's wrath, but then Jesus too became a cruel executioner of the Father's vengeance (one immediately thinks of the glowering Pantocrators of the Byzantine tradition, or Michelangelo's angry Christ in the Sistine Chapel). People then turned to Mary to intercede, and then the saints or holy relics—anything, as mercy dried up and Christian Hell intensified, while Heaven receded.

## Alternative Christians:
### Gnostics, Manicheans and Marcionians

Before Christianity became the official religion of the Roman Empire and began to persecute the competition, at the end of the 4th century, it came in more than one flavour. Every new idea and doctrine was brought out to compete with someone else's strawberry or butterscotch ripple; the word heresy actually means 'to choose', and over history hundreds of thousands were doomed to melt for choosing the wrong one.

One of the most popular heresies,

> God made the world in six days and was arrested on the seventh.
> *The Devil's Dictionary*

Prayers for the souls in Hell were strictly forbidden, and the proposed menu of joys of Heaven began to include the spectacle of torments in Hell; in hundreds of frescoes, the well-dressed, rosy-cheeked elect are depicted as pious, self-satisfied voyeurs, gazing down at the naked evil-doers writhing below. A preacher named F. W. Farrar memorably described this pleasant pastime as 'the abominable fancy' in the 19th century, by which time it began to seem rather embarassing. ❶

Gnosticism believed in a true, ultimate and transcendent God, who exists beyond all created universes, and who 'emanated' all that exists, visible and invisible. The world is divine, but imperfect because parts of this divine essence were projected so far from God that they were corrupted. The Gnostics shared a poetic creation myth: there are God-like beings called **Aeons** who perform an intermediary role between the True God and humanity. One of the Aeons, Sophia (Wisdom) in the

course of her journeyings, mistakenly desired to imitate the True God and emanated from her own being a flawed conscious being, who created the material and psychic universe out of the pre-existing divine essence, a universe shot through with his own inborn flaw. Unaware of his shabby origins, this being, the Demiurgos ('half maker'), or Blind One, imagined himself to be the one and only God.

Everyone, however, contains a divine spark, bestowed by the repentant Sophia, but most people are ignorant of the fact, thanks to the influence of the Demiurgos and his minions, the Archons, who want to keep us attached to earthly things. Death releases the divine spark from its material prison, but if the soul has not achieved a certain level of 'gnosis' (knowledge achieved by personal perception), the divine spark will be hurled back into the physical world—in other words, to Hell.

Fortunately, 'Messengers of the Light' sent from the True God help humans, including Seth (the third Son of Adam) and Jesus. For most Gnostics, Jesus is the principal saviour (Soter), not by his suffering but by his teaching; a Gnostic understands salvation as being saved from the ignorance that causes one to sin. One Gnostic tradition that passed into Merovingian France has it that Mary Magdelene was Jesus' most beloved apostle and consort; the Gnostic sacraments 'of the Bridal Chamber' led to allegations of some rather free-wheeling sexual practices.

No hanky panky touched the teachings of one Gnostic Messenger of the Light, Mani, born in Persia sometime around 215. Mani claimed to be an apostle of Jesus like Paul, and the dualist religion he preached neatly packaged Gnostic Christian elements with Zoroastriansm and Buddhism; although he was executed by puritan Zoroastrians in 276, his doctrine converted many of them, as well as most of the Gnostics. In Manicheism, the enemy of light and the True God is our old friend Ahriman, the Zoroastrian force of darkness, now linked to matter, the Demiurgos, Satan and Yaweh. It was Ahriman who created Adam and Eve, but Mani added the mischievous notion that Ahriman's intention was for Eve to use lust to seduce and tempt Adam. For a soul to reach the Realm of Light as a *perfecti* it was necessary to attain knowlege as well as live a chaste, vegetarian life, or face another reincarnation. Those who were still unredeemed at the Last Judgement would burn for 1468 years.

Although Manicheans were persecuted from the end of the 4th century, their vision of the world as a filthy rotten place (which it was, at the anarchic fall of the Roman empire) contributed to the ascetic streak in Christianity that began in the 3rd century, with the appearance of the first flesh-mortifying hermits and monks. **Augustine** (364–430), the father of western theology, was raised a Christian but converted to Manicheism for nine years before he reconverted to Christianity. The experience must have hardened his heart towards Eve, as he formulated the Doctrine of Original Sin, a doctrine used to justify the oppression of women for centuries.

Women may have done better, and Hell would certainly have been a cosier place for Christians, had Augustine flirted instead with the gentler heresy of Marcion, who shared the Gnostic idea that Yahweh was completely distinct from the God of the New Testament. A devout Christian from Pontus, Marcion went to Rome in c.140, but got himself excommunicated four years later for his belief that only Paul had truly understood the original gospel of love preached by Jesus; the other early disciples, Marcion claimed, had been corrupted by Judaizing tendencies. Following Paul, he believed in the annihilation theory for sinners, rather than a Hell to fry them in. Marcion's following grew into a sect that rivalled the Church until the gloves were taken off in the 4th century, and it was wiped out (or so the Church thought; now like every other heresy, it has its own web page).

# medieval hell

The Middle Ages were the golden age of Hell. With the collapse of the Roman empire, the end of the world seemed nigh and interest in what lay beyond was keen. And it continued at a high pitch as the Church with a capital C developed Hell as its most powerful weapon of social and political control, the force behind its endless anathemas and excommunications against individuals, ideas, cities and states. For a thousand years Hell loomed just underfoot, with all the uneasiness, threat and potential horror that the world's nuclear arsenals hold over us today, and people, even as Europe sank into feudal illiterate

107

dotage, wanted the straight poop. They were anxious; the place gave them nightmares, but like us moderns watching Dr Strangelove, they didn't mind being entertained by it, either.

After the year 1000, the world was supposed to end; as usual, it didn't, and there followed a church-building spree across Europe in the new Romanesque style. Nearly all of the new churches offered vigorous illustrations of the consquences of bad living. Last Judgements were favourites, and gratifyingly showed bishops, monks and kings boiling in pots alongside everyone else. The Archangel Michael has dusted off the ancient Egyptian soul-weighing scales, while the Hydra jaws of Tartarus described by Virgil have become the leering Hell mouth; Satan, in a mockery of the Trinity, was given three faces. The 'dark angels' from the old apocalypses evolved into proper demons, with cloven hooves, leering faces and pitchforks. The 'worms that sleepeth not' are fearsome breast- and genital-biting snakes, whose coiling defends prudery in the nether regions.

To the Hell bequeathed by Augustine, Revelations, and the apocryphal gospels, the Middle Ages added a new genre: visions, accounts of visits to Heaven and Hell by everyday people, who temporarily die or fall into a coma and revive to tell what they've seen. There are dozens of these, all on the order of modern tabloid accounts of folks being kidnapped by nefarious aliens.

Hieronymus Bosch *Tondal's Vision*

The first visions were recorded by Pope Gregory the Great in the 6th century, and other early examples appear in the Venerable Bede's *Ecclesiastical History of England* (731). But the Irish came up with the best visions, including *Saint Brendan's Voyage* (where Irish monks find islands of Hell in the Atlantic, and meet Judas Iscariot) and the most widely read of all, the *Vision of Tundal*. Written in 1149 by an Irish monk, Tundal, a naughty knight, falls into a coma during a fit of anger at a banquet, and his soul is taken on a very instructive and rather painful tour of Hell by his guardian angel. The angel not only shows him what awaits him if he doesn't change his ways, but lets him taste various torments: he has been greedy, so he is devoured by the Beast Acheron, bitten and burned; because Tundal once stole a cow, he must lead one over a bridge only as wide as a palm, studded with nails (pre-Dantesque, Hell is a confusion of narrow bridges and perilous ladders to cross and climb, over boiling lakes of pitch or valleys full of hungry monsters; in art it often looks like the children's game 'Snakes and Ladders'). Tundal has fornicated, and so he must be swallowed and defecated by a giant bird; he winds up his tour with a horrific sighting of Lucifer, here brought so low that he resembles a giant centipede with countless arms and legs, chained on a fiery grill, exhaling and inhaling sinners.

For those who couldn't enjoy the latest Hell-a-vision, there were fire and brimstone sermons and mystery plays to bring home the horrors in the Dark House. The first mystery plays appeared in the 12th century, and the most popular of these were the ones most successful in using stage tricks to bring the tortures to life. the diabolerie and toilet humour that accompanied Lucifer's fall, the temptations, and harrowing of Hell were the only popular comedy permitted until drama was secularized. Yet it was during this same 12th-century, when the Church enjoyed its maximum authority, that its be-good-or-be-damned programme first threatened to backfire like Old Nick's bottom (the firecracker fart was a popular feature in the mystery plays). In the French romance, *Aucaussin et Nicolette*, Aucaussin is threatened with eternal torment, but declares:

*What would I do in paradise?...In Paradise are only people like this: old priests, old cripples, old maimed, who hunch in front of altars and old crypts day and night, and those in ragged old cloaks and old rags, who are naked and shoeless and dying of hunger and thirst, cold and misery. They go to Paradise, and I want nothing to do with them. I want to go to Hell, for to Hell go the handsome clerks and knights who die in jousts and fine wars, and the good officers and noblemen: I want to go with them. And there go the beautiful and gracious ladies who have two or three friends besides their husbands, and there go the gold and silver and squirrel furs, and there go the harpers and tumblers and kings. With them I will go, so long as I have Nicolette, my so sweet friend, with me.*

Young Aucaussin's flippant remarks were nothing compared to the real troubles that faced the Church in the 12th and 13th centuries. Anticlericalism was rife; its princes had grown rich and worldly, and were resented by secular rulers and the rising mercantile classes. Even more threatening, many honest souls believed that the teachings of Christ had become distorted. St Francis' preachings of poverty and simplicity attracted much of this sentiment, but other people left the Church altogether and joined the Bogomils, Patarenes, Cathars and Waldenses. The Church met these heresies with a new weapon: the Holy Office, or Inquisition, founded in the 13th century: their cruel tortures and burnings at the stake offered a preview of the heretic's destiny in Hell *pour encourager les autres*.

Just when it seemed that Rome was making the devil redundant with its human barbeques, the Council of Lyon officially cut the ribbon and opened up Purgatory in 1274, in an attempt to win back hearts and minds. It was a black day for medieval Hell. Purgatory comes from the Latin *purgare*, 'to cleanse', and the Church would never admit it but Purgatory's flames are close to the chastizing fire of Origen. The idea of a temporary Hell had first been floated by Pope

Gregory in the 6th century; it even had a known entrance—in Ireland, a cave called St Patrick's Purgatory, by a 5th-century monastery on Station Island, County Donegal, that is still the site of one of Catholicism's weirdest pilgrimages. Making Purgatory official solved a number of problems: it allowed sinners a chance to expiate their sins before entering Heaven; it allowed the bereaved the chance to pray for the souls of their loved ones, and it explained the presence of ghosts. It also accounted for how souls would be spending their time between Particular and Universal Judgment, and it offered a ray of hope for unbaptized babies. Saints and martyrs could skip it, while the truly rotten went directly to Hell. Purgatory offered those who remained good Catholics a better chance of avoiding eternal damnation after death, especially as the chief intercessor was none other than the BVM herself (as in the *Apocalypse of Mary*, p. xx). Of course Purgatory also led to abuses, perhaps unique in the annals of religion: the creation of a booming market economy of afterlife speculations, with precise calculations on how many years off a dead soul could expect for each Hail Mary. Indulgences offered the chance to hedge one's own bets in the beyond, offering credit in the bank of grace through pilgrimages, acts of piety (or paying someone else to perform them in one's name) or just plain money.

## The Reformation: Damned If You Do, Damned If You Don't

Martin Luther became one of the great heroes of Hell when he slammed the door to Purgatory, threw away the key, and gave the Virgin her walking papers. Luther meant to be a law student, but when he was struck by lightning and survived he took this as a divine message to switch careers and became a monk. This firm belief in destiny coloured his reading of Paul and Augustine: Paul, almost uniquely in the New Testament, wrote of charis, or grace, which he interpreted to mean the free gift of salvation, given by God to liberate humans from sin and death 'through the redemption which is in Christ Jesus' (Romans 3:24). Augustine insisted that this grace was a free gift, given by God

without regard to human merit. But as God alone determines who will receive grace, some are predestined to salvation. The monk struck by lightning took this one step further.

The story goes that Luther was on pilgrimage in Rome, on his knees, half way up the steps of the Lateran's Sancta Sanctorum when he heard a little voice that said, 'The just shall live by faith, not by pilgrimage, not by

> it is hardly surprising that Luther had his great Protestant epiphany while sitting on the toilet

penance', whereupon he did the unthinkable: he stood up and walked back down. Back in Wittenberg in 1517, he pinned his 95 theses against the sale of indulgences on the door of the church, arguing that if only God's grace could save a soul, the Pope was the Antichrist for misleading people into thinking the Church had any post-mortem influence at all. Unfortunately, while dismissing all the saints as intercessors for the good, Luther kept all the intercessors for the bad: the demons and Satan,

created by God and predestined to fall. What he really warned against was reason. 'There is on earth among all dangers no more dangerous thing than a richly endowed and adroit reason, especially if she enters into spiritual matters which concern the soul and God. For it is more possible to teach an ass to read than to blind such a reason and lead it right; for reason must be deluded, blinded, and

destroyed.' Luther not only sent thinking people to Hell, but because he believed in demons, his severe doctrines also sent hundreds of innocent women there, brutally condemned as witches. (Luther was continually haunted by spiteful devils, and in one famous incident he threw an inkpot at one; others worked in his bowels, causing all kinds of distressing flatulence, and it is hardly surprising that Luther had his great Protestant epiphany while sitting on the toilet).

John Calvin, the second major figure of the Protestant reformation, believed in an omnipotent God's free gift of grace to the extent that it was impossible for a person to do anything to save themselves, a doctrine of double predestination affirmed by the Synod of Dort (1619) in Holland and in the Westminster Confession (1647) in England. The idea that it was God's will that a majority of His creatures be born only to be eternally punished was so attractive that it took northern Europe by storm, and through the Puritans, it landed in colonial America. The Puritans had no doubt where they were to go, and in the first great cycle of American revivals, the Great Awakening (1730s–40s), their doctrine of predestination was colourfully expressed by Jonathon Edwards, in his sermon *Sinners in the Hands of an Angry God* (1741), who unforgettably depicts God holding us on his fingers like yo-yos over the flames of Hell, suspended there at his will.

The great Hell story of the Reformation was based on a real Doctor Johannes Faust, who took a degree at Heidelberg in 1509, and worked as an astrologer and alchemist. While still alive, he attracted rumours accusing him of calling up the dead and practising black magic. It seems that he was murdered some time around 1540, not long after a story made the rounds that he had signed a pact with the devil. This appeared in the Historia von Doctor J. Faustus, published in 1587 by J. Spies: the devil, here represented by a new servant of Lucifer named Mephistopheles, granted Faust riches, knowledge, and pleasures in exchange for his soul. Translated into all European languages, the *Historia* inspired Christopher Marlowe's masterful *Tragical History of the Life and Death of Doctor Faustus* (1604).

## Baroque Hell

In the 16th century, a Protestant sect known as Ubiquists, or Ubiquitarians, led by a Swabian theologian named Johann Brenz offered a solution to the problems of infernal overcrowding by tearing down the gates and draining the Styx; their Hell, in fact, was everywhere, and the damned were allowed to go wherever they pleased in the universe, although they had to carry their punishment with them. They never said as much, but one can just imagine the damned drifting about the cosmos with camping stoves and barbeques strapped to their backs. Little known

out rather fetching with its possibili-
ties for space travel, Ubiquist Hell
gets four stars in this guidebook.
The Jesuits, in charge of Catholic
infernal affairs in the same century,
took an exactly opposite approach.
Although they preached that half of
Europe was now damned by their
Protestant heresies in the 16th and
17th centuries, rather than expand
Hell to gobble down the throngs,
they closed off all the valleys, moun-
tains and *bolgias* (the circles of
Dante's Inferno), all the levels and
rings and herded everyone into an
alarmingly claustrophobic city, citing
Nicodemus' description of Hell as the
'insatiable devourer of all things'; i.e.
it even devoured itself. All the humid-
ity, the rivers, snow and ice melted
away and dried up. The Jesuits
arranged Hell like a funnel, to collect
all the filth on earth like a sewer, but
it was a *cloaca minima*, as small as
four square miles, big enough, the
subtle doctors reckoned, to squeeze
in all of the 20 to 800 billion sinners
damned since the world was created
5000 years ago. Dante's spacious,
organized geometric Inferno, where
individuals kept their names and
received customized torments
became a tightly packed, dirty,
smelly, anonymous slum, a foetid

stew where the eschatological meet.
the scatalogical in the city of Hell
Syphilis was rampant at the tim
(Rabelais was the first to introduce
the disease down below), and this
latrine Hell was very much a suffocat
ingly overcrowded hospital for vene
real diseases.

the elect would come
out of the angelic
cookie-cutters,
beautiful, slim and
pleasantly scented

Dante's 'incontinent', those left out
side Hell proper for lack of sufficient
malice, were now belly to belly, bum
to bum, and cheek to cheek with the
worst sinners from across the social
spectrum. In swarming piles of decay
ing bodies, where it was impossible
to move without kicking, biting or
penetrating another body, the
damned themselves became demons
torturing and impregnating the peo
ple around them. Satan and his min
ions were given their walking papers
by the Jesuits: they were expendable
once Hell became other people.

In case this stinking orgy sounded
interesting to anyone, the point was

stressed that 'baker-angels' who reconstructed the body on Judgement Day would make suitable physical adjustments: the unrighteous would receive disgusting, slow, foul-smelling, and obese bodies, while the elect, even if they were ugly or deformed in life, would come out

of the angelic cookie-cutters, beautiful, slim and pleasantly scented. But that wasn't all. Everyone was burned by Hell fire, which contained every imaginable pain in every single spark.

Jesuit Hell was customized for a refined, educated and influential audience, who no longer believed in, or were no longer terrified of, medieval Hell, especially once the 16th-century Council of Trent confirmed that Purgatory was an afterlife option for Catholics. To keep the upper classes on the straight and narrow, the Jesuits made the Church's eternal Hell intolerably smelly and democratic. It was no sooner invented than life began to imitate it, in an era of bloody persecutions, tortures, inquisitions and finally the Thirty Years' War (1618–48), a pan-European power struggle so horrific that it was considered the dress rehearsal for the Apocalypse; in parts of Germany, the principal battlefield, half of the civilian population died. People flocked to cities already bursting at the seams; poverty, plagues and disease were rife, and the Hell-as-slum image became all too real. Although few artists cared to take up the challenge of depicting the dystopia of Baroque Hell, the 17th-century Genoese painter Alessandro Magnasco captured the spirit of the time in his crowded, dimly-lit scenes of wraiths, forerunners of the dark sets of films like *Metropolis* and *Blade Runner*.

As the cruel century progressed, so did the idea that God found the tortures of the damned amusing.

Tertullian, in the 2nd century, was the first to describe the elect as voyeurs, piously gloating as they peered down to watch the torments of Hell, but now God Himself couldn't stop laughing. 'Justice has ascended to God. He doesn't stop watching with pleasure the wretches whom he has chased into the fire suffer from their torments, and while gazing at them he laughs,' wrote the discalced Augustinian preacher Angelo Maria Quadrio, and the times were so awful that no one disagreed. The howling souls of the damned cascading in flames were a nightly fireworks show for Heaven's amusement.

The overcrowded overheated slum Hell, with its merciless fire and unbearable smells, minus devils, geographical features, and individualized torture service, was adopted by most Protestant sects in the theological arms race. It was preached in hair-raising detail by the priest in James Joyce's *Portrait of the Artist as a Young Man*, in a sermon Joyce was able to reproduce from memory. When Emanuel Swedenborg had his visions in the 18th century, he went down in a lift and found innumerable Hells, one for each sin, with a matching Heaven for each one; some were Jesuit Hells, 'ruins of houses and cities after conflagrations, in which infernal spirits dwell and hide themselves. In the milder Hells there is an appearance of rude huts, in some cases contiguous in the form of a city with lanes and streets, and within the houses are infernal spirits engaged in unceasing quarrels, enmities,

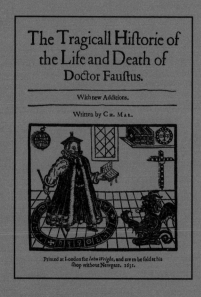

fightings, and brutalities; while in the streets and lanes robberies and depredations are committed. In some of the Hells there are nothing but brothels, disgusting to the sight and filled with every kind of filth and excrement.'

It was all wretched enough to keep a keen edge on Faustian bargains. Tirso de Molina's *El Burlador de Sevilla* (1630) introduced Don Juan to the world, the refined, cynical nobleman who fulfills a long list of male fantasies before meeting the statue that flings him down to the filth and flames. After seeing Marlowe's *Faust* performed in a German puppet show, Goethe came up with the best seller, *Faust*, Part I, was published in 1808, and added the love story of Faust and Margarete to the legend. Goethe kept *Faust*, Part 2, locked up until after his death, and when it was published in 1832, everyone was shocked to find that he had changed the ending: Margarete intervenes and saves Faust's soul.

Hector Berlioz in turn was inspired by Goethe to compose his musical drama, *La Damnation de Faust*. He keeps the love story but sends Faust to Hell, on the way writing the best infernal music in the classical repertoire, as he and the suave Mephistopheles thunder off to the Abyss, Faust wails in despair, demons grab his soul and burst into a triumphant song in an infernal language invented for the purpose by Berlioz: '*Has! Irimirukarabrao! Has! Has! Has!*

# hell Today

*I remember an old woman looking with the jealousy of poverty and age at a young English officer, who was passing by on horseback, handsomely accoutred. 'Ah!' said she, 'for all his lace he goes to Hell.' A priest standing by reproved her presumption, by calling her a beast, a favourite Italian phrase, 'Che siete bestia'—'as for the Turks,' continued he, 'they certainly go to Hell, but nobody knows where the English go.'*

William Irvine,
*Letters on Sicily, 1813*

Well, these days they don't go anywhere. In January 1996, Doctrine Commission of the Church of England's *The Mystery of Salvation* obliterated Hell, by redefining it as 'annihilation for all who reject the love of God', with the comment that 'Christians have professed appalling theologies which made God into a sadistic monster and left searing psychological scars on many.' Even so, according to a recent Gallup poll, 24% of Britons say they still believe in Hell.

Is Hell really going up in smoke? Most people think that God isn't bad

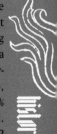

> 'Hell is other people' and no one familiar with Parisians would be surprised at Sartre's conclusion

enough to send anyone there anymore, and that we ourselves aren't bad enough to deserve it. 'Hell would frankly be wasted on a population of sandwich-eaters,' states Italian infernologist Piero Camporesi in *The Fear of Hell*, adding, 'The Hell of the five senses is no longer buried down there in "the heart of the earth". And even if it has transferred itself up here, among us, we do not even notice it.' Few people protested too much when Sartre proclaimed 'Hell is other people', or even when TS Eliot disagreed and said 'Hell is oneself.' Sartre, of course, lived in Paris, and no one familiar with Parisians would be surprised at his conclusion; if half the things people said about Eliot were really true, his opinion too would be quite indisputable.

In the literature of the last 200 years, Hell is hardly ever deemed worth a visit, though the Devil has enjoyed continued popularity. Usually he is a modern, sophisticated Mephistophelian Devil, a sensual and witty *boulevardier* like the one in Baudelaire's story *The Generous Gambler*. In *Man and Superman*, George Bernard Shaw conjures up a Devil in much the same vein, only more windy and Shavian:

> *I don't admire the Heavenly temperament: I don't understand it. I don't know that I particularly want to understand it, but it takes all sorts to make a universe...*

There are plenty of others. Tennyson wrote a play about the Devil when he was fourteen years old. Writers from Robert Louis

## Hell would frankly be wasted on a population of sandwich-eaters
*Piero Camporesi*

Robert De Niro plays
a soul-purchasing
Mephisto to a T
down in the Bible Belt

Cinema provided a chance to add a new dimension to the infernal chronicles, but so far few have taken up the challenge. The film *Dante's Inferno*, in the 1960s, was merely a vehicle to show lots of naked women and whips; the Antichrist features in *The Devil's Advocate*, where Satan (Al Pacino) runs a big law firm in New York Hell and tries to get his son to take the role. In *Angel Heart*, Robert De Niro plays a soul-purchasing Mephisto to a T down in the Bible Belt. But in the history of cinema, these are rarities; the Devil just doesn't sell, Hollywood says, and even with their best special effects it would be difficult to make a Hell capable of impressing today's jaded audiences.

Horror films, essentially escapist, have done their best to avoid the Devil and all the cultural baggage he carries; they prefer vampires, or mad scientists, and only the dimmest Killer B's are given a Satanist angle. But the tradition of the old Devil

Stevenson to Guy de Maupassant built little moral tales around him, and he was always a favourite with the Russians, as in Dostoevsky's *The Possessed*, or *The Devil and St John's Eve* by Gogol—in most Russian literature, really, he's never far away. The Americans made a mildly profitable cottage industry out of Devil stories. Washington Irving lets the Old Deceiver win a round in *The Devil and Tom Walker*, while the tables are turned in that high-school anthology standby, *The Devil and Daniel Webster* by Stephen Vincent Benet, in which his eminence is outwitted by a United States Senator (the last time that ever happened). In James Branch Cabell's *Jurgen*, he is a wry, world-weary bureaucrat, but one who grants Jurgen enough favours for the book to be banned in Boston.

short story lives on in the modern genre of morality tales with a supernatural twist, invented by Poe and best exemplified in our times by television series' like *The Twilight Zone*.

This, and other shows like it, achieved the ultimate in the trivialization of Hell. One memorable episode, back in the 1960s, has one of Hell's Angels arriving in the pit, where he is met by a rather bland devil. The biker gleefully rubs his hands, asking for the promised pitchforks, chains and fires, but when the devil shows him the door to Hell, it turns out to be a room with a man showing and narrating home movies of his family vacations. For ever and ever... Another episode portrayed Hell as a pool room, where a new arrival who was a great pool shark on earth is alone with a legendary past champion whom he must defeat. Eventually he does, but he soon realizes that his doom is to wait there, for centuries if necessary, until someone comes along who can beat him. The message of most of these ironic tales is clear, and it is confirmed by every study that asks the man on the street his opinion on what Hell would be like— to the modern mind, Hell is nothing more or nothing less than eternal boredom.

# The Last True Believers

°Judgement Day!!!
°PUNISHMENT AND DAMNATION TO THE WICKED!!!!!
°HELL-FIRE to the INFIDEL!!!
°Hosanna in the HIGHEST!!!

> —from the website of the Prophet Jonas, of Nederland, Colorado.

Hell, the ultimate Rocky Horror Show, has had a very long run, and like all cult shows it survives longer in some places than others. It may have disappeared from most Europeans'

> Hell, the ultimate Rocky Horror Show, has had a very long run, and like all cult shows it survives longer in some places than others.

cosmologies, but according to one poll 60% of Americans still say they believe in Hell. Interestingly, only 5% think they are destined to see it (but then, 80% of all Americans think of themselves as above-average drivers). Americans from the beginning have had an intimate relationship with Old

Nick and his Kingdom and, more remarkably, from the beginning they have done their best to reproduce it here on earth.

The first British colonists in North America found a beautiful and unspoiled continent, with bluebirds singing in the trees in an unbroken stretch from the Atlantic coast to the Mississippi. Naturally, they were scared to death of it. And since most of them, especially in New England, were quivering religious crackpots, they quickly concluded that the sole purpose of the glories around them was to deceive them, to tempt them from the paths of Righteousness. Nature, quite simply, was the work of the Devil. Just ask Cotton Mather:

*The New Englanders are a people of God settled in those, which were once the Devil's Territories; and it may be supposed that the Devil was exceedingly disturbed, when he perceived such a People here accomplishing the Promise of old made unto our Blessed Jesus.... I believe, that never were more Satanical Devices used for the Unsettling of any People under the Sun, than what have been here Employ'd for the Extirpation of the Vine which God has here Planted, Casting out the Heathen, and preparing a Room before it, and causing it to take deep Root, and fill the Land...An Army of Devils is horribly broke in upon the place which is the Center, and after a sort, the First-born of our English Settlements; and the Houses of Good People there are fill'd with the doleful Shrieks of their Children and Servants, Tormented by Invisible Hands, with Tortures altogether preternatural.*

—from The Wonders of the Invisible World

Like Adam in the Garden, the colonists in the American wilderness had the job of bestowing names on the things they saw. So one of the prettiest flowers of the eastern meadows, the orange hawkweed, became the 'Devil's paintbrush', joining a dozen or so other diabolically-inspired flower names in New World botany. And as the settlers moved ever westwards, wherever they went they found that the Devil had always been there before them. Difficult river bends became the Devil's Elbow, rapids the Devil's Chute or Devil's Raceway. The Old Enemy was reasserting control in both urban and rural milieus; a patch of rocky soil, or a city-centre slum could be called a Devil's Half-Acre or Hell's Half-Acre. Missouri, a state particularly rich in diabolic geography, knows a Devil's Backbone, a Devil's Tea Table, Devil's Tollgate and the Devil's Washbasins.

Florida has not only devilfish and a vine called devil's shoestring, but sinkholes called the Devil's Punch Bowl and the Devil's Mill Hopper. Along the Mississippi River, at a place in Louisiana called Batture du Diable by the French and Devil Flats by the English, voodoo zombies were said to walk. The Devil has indeed left his mark in all fifty states—even more so out West, where the landscapes encourage it. As for the real Hell, folks carefully and politely would choose not to mention it, preferring circumlocutions like Sam Hill, Jo and Tarnation.

The most Hellacious place in the entire US is undoubtedly New York City, with Hell Gate, the Spuyten Duyvil, and of course that sylvan corner of Manhattan called Hell's Kitchen, where the old warehouses are currently filling up fast with childless yuppies; the neighborhood association there proudly proclaims to the world that 'This is the neighborhood your grandmother warned you about.' Hell's Kitchen, incidentally, was originally Heil's Kitchen, named after a long-ago German couple who ran a country inn and served up good beer and knockwurst, but in America the cachet of infernal connections was always too attractive. Innocent Germans were also behind Hell, Michigan, a pleasant little town near Detroit from which you can send home a 'Howdy from Hell' postcard. At that latitude, Hell freezes over faithfully every winter.

Hell-haunted America isn't really that different from other lands. Americans are simply more likely to think in terms of metaphor, which at times can be helpful both in art and public policy. Even Europeans, who like to sweep things under the rug, might agree that it's good to have a nation obsessed with the presence of Evil when there's a Hitler or a Stalin in the neighborhood. In addition, America is always there to provide sophisticates a source of entertainment, with some of the most extravagant religious craziness the world has seen since St Simeon Stylites climbed up on his pillar.

The 1980s was a decade that saw America at its silliest, a time when the county government of Kleberg County, Texas, was urging its people to stand up for God by answering the telephone 'Heaven-o!' instead of the infernal alternative. A few years ago even the Rev Jerry Falwell noted that the cynical tenor of the times, and the well-publicized indiscretions of some preachers, were 'making it harder and

harder for Christians to sit down and write those checks'. These days, even the radio and television preachers don't like to talk about Hell more than is necessary. Most of them discovered long ago that you get more cheques by making people feel good about themselves than you do by browbeating them with threats of Eternal Fire.

For the real old-time religion, these days you have to go to the same place

*...the horror of HELL is NOT only for those who are the Mass murderers, or Hitler, or the really Evil of this world but Hell is filled with people we love, and our neighbors and friends who give to Charities, always there to lend a helping hand.*

Reverend Sherrie also asks us to pray for 'a Christian Web Manager that will NOT try and control what the Holy Spirit tells me to do.'

# eternity is forever

the Satanists hang out—the internet. The Reverend Sherrie, at the Alpha & Omega Almighty Wind Holy Ghost Fire Church (*www.almightywind.com/realHell.htm*), reminds us cheerfully that 'Eternity is Forever!' Reverend Sherrie voices an argument common among serious hell-raisers since Jonathan Edwards: no matter how virtuous you think you might be, just one false step, one moment of weakness, and you're doomed. So most of us, when we finally make it to Hell, will feel right at home:

Outside the internet, you can find the same sentiments expressed in many of America's art museums. In 1976, Howard Finster, a 60-year-old tent revivalist preacher and bicycle repairman from Alabama, was touching up some scratches on a bike when he had a vision: a human face appeared in the paint dripping from his finger and told him to paint 'sacred art'. Full of missionary zeal, Finster has done just that, not illustrating stories from the Bible but producing what he calls 'sermons in

paint,' often depictions from his own visions of other worlds, especially Hell, a weird and awful place, complete with demons, firebreathing serpents, and most terrifying of all, the Hellhound of old, Cerberus now a harmless, banal-looking dog, in a

new interpretations of the Book of Revelations is high on the list of the most popular national pastimes, falling roughly between stock-car racing and slow-pitch softball. A diligent and weary Christian journalist named William Alnor, who follows these

Santa Claus hat. These are accompanied by Finster's warnings: 'THOSE WHO DON'T BELIEVE IN HELL WILL WIND UP IN HELL', 'HELL IS A HELL OF A PLACE', and 'NO COLD COKES'.

Americans, crazy or not, tend to care more for spectacles than philosophy. And for at least the last few decades, the prophets of fire and brimstone have been less concerned with Hell itself than with the big event that will usher in the end of this fallen world: the Apocalypse. Finding

things (in a book called *Soothsayers of the Second Advent*), calls the game 'pinning the tail on the Antichrist'. Frequently-mentioned candidates for this position have included not only that old favourite, the Pope, but also Henry Kissinger, Jimmy Carter, Pat Robertson, Willy Brandt, Prince Charles, Mikhail Gorbachev, and Karl von Habsburg, pretender to the Austro-Hungarian throne.

Why so many Europeans? It's a common theme among aficionados;

according to them Revelations foresaw the European Union, and names its creation as an evil undertaking that heralds the Final Days. Other preachers harp on about the Middle East, where they expect a new 'Messiah' (who's really the Antichrist)

to arise in Israel. 1988 was supposed to be the big year, and one Apocalyptic prophet was selling tours to Jerusalem for a front-row seat:

*We stay at the Intercontinental Hotel right on the Mount of Olives where you can get the beautiful view of the Eastern Gate and the Temple Mount. And if this is the year of our Lord's return, as we anticipate, you may even ascend to Glory from within a few feet of his Ascension.*

Current Apocalypse theory is particularly concerned with the nefarious

Federal Government, and its plans to achieve an even closer control of its citizens in preparation for the Antichrist's coming. There's a lot of talk about the 'Mark of the Beast' (Rev. 13: 16, 17)—first this was supposed to be supermarket bar codes,

> Finding new interpretations of the Book of Revelations is high on the list of the most popular national pastimes

and now the tabloids are screaming that the government plans to implant chips with identification codes under Americans' skins. According to the Free Internet Church of Philadelphia (*www.escape666.com*),

*Bible Prophecy even foretold of the coming change in our monetary system; to a global credit-card system! Cash money will be VOID and unless you embrace a Religion of Satanism (666) you cannot buy or sell anything: no food, no water, no clothing, no medicine; nothing!*

They may be on to something there. When the government starts fooling with cash money, the world will truly be going to Hell in a handcart. So far, even though some Americans may spend their lives jumping out of bed for Apocalyptic false alarms, at least they can enjoy the satisfaction of knowing that Hell will always be with them. It's a part of America, as much as the Blue Ridge, the Badlands, the Back Bay, the Hudson Valley or the Knob Country of Old Kentuck'.

## L'Envoi

At the beginning of the current age, we all might have been spared a lot of foolishness if people had listened to the Roman philosopher Lucretius. A follower of Epicurus, who wrote his classic *On the Nature of the Universe* in the time of Julius Caesar, Lucretius proposed a rational, strangely modern approach to explaining the world around us. Christianity was not yet born, but every other sort of cult was already seeping in from the east, corroding the classical Greek spirit as they filled men's minds with supernatural visions. All through his long, serene philosophical poem, Lucretius seems haunted by premonitions of the Hell that was soon to come,

*You yourself, if you surrender your judgement at any time to the blood-curdling declamations of the prophets, will want to desert our ranks. Only think what phantoms they can conjure up to overturn the tenor of your life and wreck your happiness with fear. And not without cause. For, if men saw that a term was set to their troubles, they would find strength in some way to withstand the hocus-pocus and intimidations of the prophets. As it is, they have no power of resistance, because they are haunted by the fear of eternal punishment after death. They know nothing of the nature of the soul.*

But what about the nature of evil, then? One of the most recent public statements of the Old Enemy himself comes courtesy of Leszek Kolakowski, in an essay entitled 'A Shorthand Transcript of a Metaphysical Press Conference Given by the Devil in Warsaw, on 20 December 1963'.

Kolakowski, a dour Polish philosopher, gives us a dour Polish Devil, one who states his case dryly and dispassionately, and who proves surprisingly willing to explain in detail just what devilry he's been up to. The Devil says he visits churches to hear the sermons; he is constantly surprised that nobody ever mentions him.

The Devil also offers some intriguing tips on how he goes about his evil work. It's a prosaic, everyday business. His work is 'arid, and without